invite
PRESS

THE PRESENT PASTOR

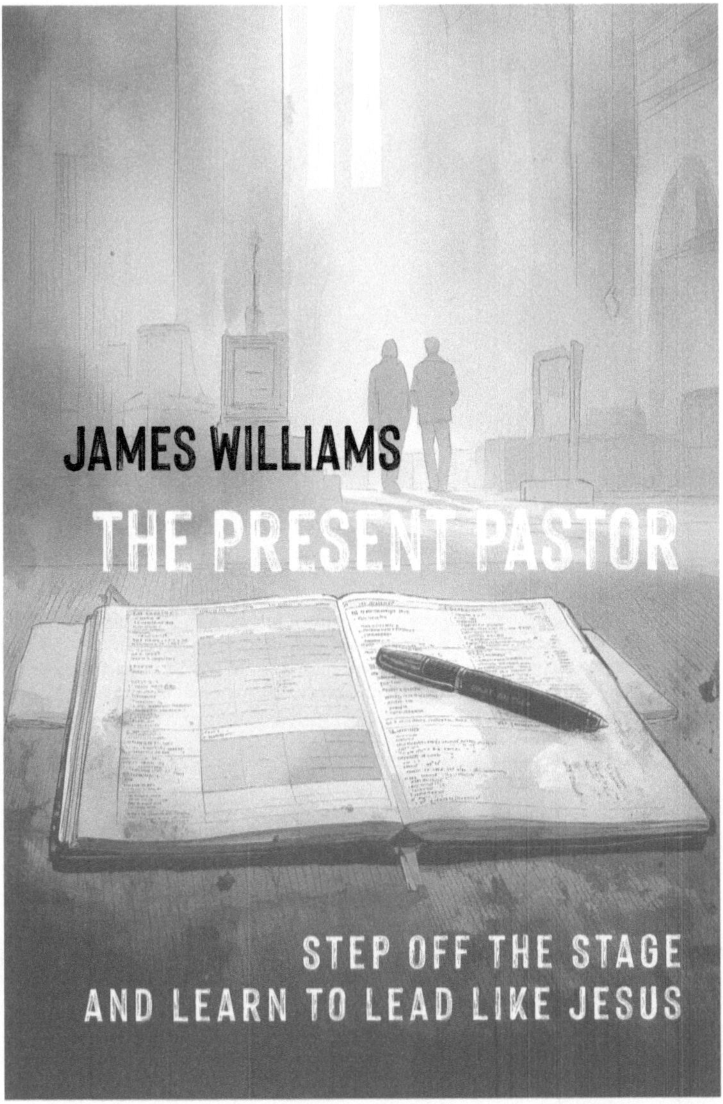

JAMES WILLIAMS

THE PRESENT PASTOR

STEP OFF THE STAGE AND LEARN TO LEAD LIKE JESUS

Plano, Texas

DEDICATION

Dedications are always incomplete. There are so many people I could thank, people who've impacted my life, shaped my journey, and walked with me through both joy and sorrow. If your name doesn't appear here, please know that I still carry deep gratitude for you in my heart. To the main editor of this work, Jessica Barber-Brown of Invite Press, thank you for your encouragement, kindness and patience. This book absolutely would not have happened without your thoroughness, skill and many clarion calls to "get it done!" I would be remiss if I did not thank the dear congregation of Grace Resurrection Church in East Cobb, Georgia. You have been used to teach, love, and heal me in so many ways. Your kindness is absolutely one of the most miraculous things I've ever experienced. I'm extremely blessed. God has been so good to me, and this book is a testament to that goodness.

First and foremost, I dedicate this book to my first true love after Jesus, the love of my life, the mother of my children, and my partner in ministry—Natalie. You are one of the most compassionate, loving people I've ever known. Your nonjudgmental spirit and your genuine love for every person God places in your path have inspired me in ways you'll never fully understand. I'm a better man because you are in my life. I will be forever grateful to God for the blessing He gave me the day I saw you for the very first time. I love and adore you.

To my children, John and Mary Grace, you are two of the unsung heroes of this book. I haven't said much about you out of respect for your privacy, but both of you are among the kindest, most loyal, and intelligent people I know. Your love for me has healed places in my soul I didn't know were broken. Watching you grow from beautiful babies to beautiful adults who love people and love Jesus has been the greatest honor of my life. Thank you for calling me "Dad."

To my mother-in-law, Patty—you've been a beacon to me more times than I can count. You were the mother I never had. You've been endlessly patient, fiercely supportive, and full of grace. Thank you for being a living example of Proverbs 31 and a gift to our entire family. Your compassion and dignity will live on through them for many generations to come.

To Carlisle Stevenson—teachers from days gone by rarely get the recognition they deserve. Thank you for your patience, kindness, and encouragement in spite of my aloof, unkind, and disrespectful attitude as a thirteen-year-old boy. You were the first person to ever communicate the potential you saw in me. You were Christ to me and believed in me, and because of your example, I've survived and have spent my life trying to pay it forward. You absolutely made a difference in this life. And to top it all off, you're a good Methodist! God bless you.

To Bishop Al Gwinn—the first time I saw you, I was intimidated. You were a towering presence in Kentucky Methodism, and I assumed your kindness from the stage must be too good to be true. But then you became my supervisor and very quickly my friend. Your authenticity, your unwavering love for Jesus Christ, and your support through both bright days and dark ones will remain one of the greatest blessings of my life. You not only believed in me, but you also walked with me. When I grow up, I want to be like you!

To Jane Ferry, I'll never forget your voice on my answering machine in 1995. I was about to leave everything behind in South Carolina and move to Kentucky, and you called to say you'd be my congregation's lay leader. I had no idea then that you'd become one of the greatest friends Natalie and I have ever had. Thank you for your unconditional love, support, and undying belief in us.

To Dr. Scott Baker—one of the dearest friends I've ever known. You are one of the wisest people in my life. Your brilliance is only matched by your compassion and faithfulness. You've walked with me through confusion and clarity, through storms and seasons of peace, not to mention we've rung in the New Year together the past twenty-five years! Your family is my family. You've helped shape every chapter of this book in one way or another. Keep fighting. Thank you for being my friend.

To Dr. Esther Jadhav, I remember sitting in my office as a new District Superintendent when you first walked in and introduced yourself. I thought, "This is one of the most intelligent people I've ever met." I was right. I was your "boss," but you led me! You became a trusted friend and colleague, someone whose passion for justice, love for young people, and deep trust in the Lord have inspired me again and again. Thank you for your courage, your prayers, your clear, Christian witness, and for sharing your brilliance and your trust with me. When I do or say something dumb, I always hear your voice in my head saying, "Oh, James!"

To the Rev. Mary Eskew Rowell, though you're now a part of the great cloud of witnesses, this book wouldn't be complete without mentioning your love, pastoral care, and determination that I was going to answer my call. You taught me everything I know about church planting, and I'm honored to have worked by your side as you helped birth a beautiful, new Methodist congregation in 1992. It's going strong today because of your sleepless nights, difficult work, and faithfulness. I'm now honored to be planting a new church thirty-five years later, and I think of you almost daily.

To Zach Davis, Chris Banner, Zach Meerkreebs, Aaron Mansfield, Taylor Bacon, Billy Kenney, Jimmie Roper, Garrett Fahrbach, Wilkes Riggins, Neil Janes, and Derek Warnick—you are all younger than I am, but I have looked up to you in so many ways. Your wisdom, your character, your Christ-centered integrity, and your friendships have shaped me. Each of you has been an Onesiphorus to me (2 Timothy 1:16). You have "often refreshed me and [were] not ashamed of my chains." You give me great hope for the future of the church.

And to Dr. Randy Mickler—thank you for trusting me with a bold and precious vision that God gave you. You became a mentor and a friend so quickly. Your love for people and your unwavering devotion to Christ are unmatched. You built and led one of the largest, most vital, and most effective congregations in Methodism, and I'm honored to take over the reins as we launch this new ministry in East Cobb. I believe with all my heart that it will touch the world with the love of Christ and the Wesleyan Way.

With deep gratitude,
James Williams

TABLE OF CONTENTS

PREFACE

"In a weak moment, I wrote a book."

In one of her first interviews after becoming the famous author of *Gone with the Wind*, Margaret Mitchell was asked how she came to write such a story. She replied with that off-the-cuff line. It resonates with me. In my early years of ministry, I would never have even attempted to write a book. I was too strong, too busy, and too driven for the things of God to take that kind of time.

But a few years ago, something shifted in me. It wasn't burnout. It wasn't disappointment in the church. It wasn't even exhaustion. It was confusion—confusion about what the local church is and what it's really called to be.

I was praying without answers. I had a behind the scenes, front row seat to the implosion of the United Methodist Church. As a second-career pastor who loves the church with all of my heart and soul, a denominational leader, and delegate to the General Conference, it was like watching a train wreck with cars full of innocent people. I felt helpless and ill equipped to save the folks on the train. All I could do was watch it crash and burn. And I wasn't telling anyone my jaded thoughts about the denomination to which I had dedicated my life. So, in a moment of weakness, I started writing. I'd write a few pages, then stop for months. Sometimes I stopped because it was too painful, and other times, I was busy being super pastor to many who unbelievably allowed me to think I was just that. Friends would ask, "How's the book coming?" That would get me going again.

And now, here it is.

This isn't as long or as dramatic as *Gone with the Wind,* but it is honest. Everything you'll read is from my perspective. No doubt, I've forgotten something or have chosen to leave it out to "protect the innocent." It's my story, and I'm sticking to it. God has revealed Himself to me in ways that are so very hard to put into words, but this is my way of honoring God and trying to help others avoid some of the bumps and bruises of ministry. These pages are a raw account of my life and ministry, an unfiltered journal of calling, darkness, light, struggle, joy, and transformation. It's in no way the whole story or about any one event or person. It's a bit of wisdom made up of a conglomerate of many years, parishioners, and colleagues. All of them taught me something, and there's not one, *not one,* that I don't thank God for daily.

If you're a pastor or church leader, you'll probably find pieces of yourself here. If you're not, I hope this gives you insight into the invisible battles so many ministers quietly fight. If you're a person who has a pastor in your life that you love, this book will hopefully give you greater compassion and some tools to help you walk alongside and love him or her better. No matter how skilled or disciplined, every pastor needs a lifeboat full of a few people who love them no matter what. A wise bishop once told me that no one can truly understand a pastor's life except another pastor. It's so true. My prayer is that my story will shed some light on that truth so that the reader can grow closer to Christ and maybe learn to hold the arms up of the spiritual leader in their lives.

One experience has stuck with me for decades. Early in my ministry, I was racing out of the church door, heading somewhere I deemed "important." I bumped into a parishioner—a single mother of a severely disabled child, who had lived a life filled with trauma. She had known years of abuse not only from family but as a victim forced into prostitution. God had transformed her life, and I was so inspired by her faith. She grabbed my arm, looked me in the eyes, and said, "When are you going to stop running, James? You're always in a rush."

Her words have echoed in my spirit ever since.

This book is my attempt to stop running. To be still. To be known. To share the truth. To be fully present.

I pray it helps you do the same.

Now, let's begin.

SCARS

Just as Jesus' scars didn't disappear after his resurrection, our emotional or physical scars tell our story and lend credence to our testimony of God's love and power.

—Michelle Bengston

You might roll your eyes, as I often do, when a book starts with the writer's birth into "a log cabin in the dead of winter!" But my birth is important to the story of my call to ministry. It wasn't winter, it was fall, and it wasn't in a log cabin, but it was probably as small as one! I was born at the tail end of the 1960s, a time of cultural change, civil unrest, and rising hope that the world could somehow heal itself. But inside the walls of my childhood home, healing felt like a distant dream. My parents were young when they married, far too young to carry the weight of each other's histories. My mother came from a deeply abusive background; my father came from a home of structure and emotional restraint. Their worlds collided, not in harmony but in chaos.

They had been married for just about a year when my mother became pregnant with me. That pregnancy added pressure to an already volatile foundation. To make things more stressful, I was born with severe bilateral clubbed feet, a condition that would lead to twelve surgeries before I turned thirteen. I don't remember a time in my early life when I wasn't recovering, learning to walk again, or enduring pain that other children never knew.

While other kids ran freely, I learned to walk through pain. And not just physical pain. Emotional pain was a constant companion. Growing up in the South has been described by some as almost living in another country. It definitely has a culture of all of its own. I would not have traded that experience for the world, but between the sometimes indirect and passive ways many communicate, and the interesting dynamics that come from being in the Bible belt, I learned to read between the lines, observe carefully, and shield my emotions from an early age. I'm not sure when or why my mother declared a cold war on those who were closest to her, but I do know that there were at least two casualties: my sister and me. My parents' love faded as their fighting increased, and by the time I was five years old, my mother decided to take me and leave my father. When I think about it, my picture is being thrown over her shoulder, just another item in her carpet bag, and off we went into a whirlwind of the 1970s drug culture. The portal to that life was in the living room of our tiny, green house in rural South Carolina.

I can still see the moment in my mind: my father kneeling in front of me, a five-year-old with a deep admiration for the two most important people in my life, who were constantly locked in combat with one another. My dad, a strong and determined law enforcement officer, barely twenty-five years old, was weeping, trying to hold onto something that was slipping away. Holding both of my arms so tight I can still feel his large hands, he said, "I love you. I don't want this divorce. I'll miss you." My almost six-year-old mind had no idea what it all meant, but as often happened, a harsh, angry, barely coherent voice cut through the moment that will always be seared in my mind. Behind my father stood my mother, yelling, accusing, and demanding we go. "He doesn't love you!" she screamed. "Don't listen to him!" The next moment, we pulled out of the driveway one last time in an old, white 1965 Dodge Coronet that I spent many nights in over the next few weeks. It would be years before I reconnected with my father. For nearly two decades, I saw him only occasionally, and even when he re-entered my life as an adult, our relationship never felt fully repaired.

After we left, life unraveled even more. We had no money. My mother took a job in a department store, but her relationships and her life became increasingly unstable. She began dating different men, many of whom were abusive in various ways and in the same chaotic drug and alcohol culture that promised excitement, community, and free love.

We bounced around the South, living in every southeastern state except Louisiana. I was in twelve different elementary schools between first and sixth grade. I tell people I was raised by a bunch of hippies—not the peaceful kind you see on vintage posters but the kind deeply immersed in a lifestyle of unbelievable risks and mental health breakdowns that go after not just the physical body but the very soul. I lived where marijuana and other terrible, hallucinogenic substances were present like furniture. I saw things no child should ever see, and I carried confusion no child should ever have to carry.

Within months of leaving my father, my mother became pregnant with my sister. She married my stepfather soon after. He, too, was abusive, threatening, controlling, addicted, and dangerous. I often accompanied him on drug runs from Mexico and Florida. Underneath my bed were stored all types of illegal drugs, paraphernalia, and firearms. I can't say some of it didn't feel like an adventure to my young mind at times, but the thrill would turn into terror in an instant when my stepfather would decide to abuse me mercilessly for no reason at all. I watched our life erode to the point that my sister and I lived in constant fear of my mother dying in the midst of terrible, abusive fights. One night, I was awakened by my mother, the familiar smell of alcohol on her breath telling me to stuff as many of my things as I could into a plastic trash bag. I took no clothes. Just toys and comic books. I watched my mother stuff our little, powder-blue Ford Pinto to the gills. In a surreal fit of rage, she then grabbed a large butcher knife and began stabbing their king-sized waterbed where my passed-out stepfather was sleeping. I watched water flood our little apartment, and with my two-year-old sister, wearing only her diaper, on my back, we quickly escaped in the middle of the night, driven by fear that he would follow through on his threats if he woke up. We drove for hours into the night until I awakened the next morning in the parking lot of a southern destination for most people in the deep South, Piggly Wiggly. My mother went in, stole food for us, and we took off again, headed toward our new life. I never saw my stepfather again.

Through all of that chaos, and there was much more, I somehow never doubted that God was real.

I can't tell you I prayed, at least not in the way we talk about prayer now, but I talked to Him. I believed He was there. Even as a boy, I had a quiet awareness that there was "someone" with me, even if no one else stayed. I didn't grow up discipled, churched, or spiritually trained, but I was spiritually aware. And that awareness kept me alive, emotionally and spiritually.

But the abuse didn't stop. My mother's addictions deepened. She became increasingly violent toward me and my sister. Her neglect was painful. She was functional—working and socializing—but behind closed doors, she could be terribly cruel.

One of my most painful memories happened on Christmas morning in 1978.

We were living in Albany, Georgia. I was ten years old, and though my innocence was long gone, amazingly I still believed in Santa Claus and couldn't wait for Christmas morning. That year, I had taken the Sears catalog and circled one thing: a Huffy bicycle called "The Bandit." I just knew I'd get that sleek, black and red Cadillac of bikes that year. My mother tucked us into bed on Christmas Eve, told us Santa wouldn't come if we didn't go straight to sleep, and left into the night for a Christmas Eve party. I woke up alone with my sister on Christmas morning. No presents under the tiny, withering tree. No warmth in the house. No sign of my mother.

She had drank too much to make it home. It was the worst Christmas of my life.

Hours passed. The silence was deafening. Finally, around two in the afternoon, I heard a knock at the door. It was my schoolteacher, Mrs. Harris, accompanied by another teacher. They had brought me a gift: a brand new, bright yellow bicycle with a banana seat. I can still see it. It was beautiful.

They asked where my mother was. I lied and said she had gone to the store and would be back soon. I didn't want them to know the truth. They stayed for a while and watched as I rode my new bike around the yard in my bare feet. It was warm that Christmas, as it often is in Georgia. They eventually left, but I knew they saw the truth in my eyes.

Later that day, someone dropped my mother off. She stumbled in with a grocery bag of toys and told me that Santa had given them to her at the party. We never spoke about it again. But I never forgot it.

Every year when Christmas Eve comes around, I step into the pulpit and become not little "Jamie" but Pastor James. For years, I told no one about what happened. I had an aunt who knew the story ask me after I'd been in ministry a few years how I dealt with those many Christmas traumas being in ministry. I gave a good, super pastor answer: "I no longer think like a child. God is good." I meant it, but I lied. There hasn't been a Christmas Eve in all my years of ministry that I haven't shed a few tears in my office before walking out on a stage to sometimes preach to over 2,000 people. Maybe it's what fueled me. I believed every word I've ever preached. But there were moments that I had to push down the dark, tattered, shameful memories of the past. I was always blessed to pastor good, strong churches. They all had their own personalities, problems, and challenges. As I'd look out over the sea of kind, affluent parishioners on one of the holiest nights of the year, I could sometimes, if only in my mind, pretend that my life was like theirs. I could never let them know about the pain. I was a healer! The healer doesn't need to be healed.

But I wasn't healed. I did still think like a child. My wife and children often saw the real James on those nights when I would grow quiet and somber. I can hear Natalie now, in a beautifully decorated home with all the marvelous smells of Christmas, asking "Are you ok, honey?" Of course I was ok. How dare she ask that question of a successful pastor on a night like Christmas Eve. I had just preached to a packed sanctuary, three or four times about the "light in the darkness." Yet sometimes, in my heart, I believed that light was for my parishioners and not for me. So, I'd smile, catch myself, and try to be the dad and husband my family deserved. But that Christmas morning too often played like an old skipping, vinyl record. I remembered that empty house, that empty morning. For years, the memory brought shame and sadness. But now, with time, prayer, and the healing hand of God, I look back with a different lens.

I see a little boy who was never abandoned by God, even when everyone else failed.

I see how He sent teachers, family, and neighbors to show me kindness.

I see how He planted seeds of strength that would one day become the backbone of my ministry.

I see how He kept His hand on me and never let go.

I don't know all the "why's" of my early pain. But I know this: God was forming a shepherd, not in the safety of stained-glass sanctuaries but in the wilderness of real life.

Pastor or Christian leader, if you're reading this and your early story is more broken than beautiful, take heart, as Jesus used to say, or cheer up! You're not disqualified. You're not damaged goods. You're not too far behind.

In fact, you're right on time.

Present pastors are not polished ones.

They are the ones who know how to minister from their scars.

They are the one who know how to sit with pain because they've lived it.

They are the ones who know how to pray because they've had to.

One of the most difficult parts of my early life, something that once felt like a limitation, a burden, even a source of shame, has now become one of my greatest blessings.

As I mentioned before, I was born with bilateral clubbed feet, a condition that caused my heel cords to be extremely tight and short, preventing my heels from touching the ground. It took years of surgeries, casts, braces, and even times in a wheelchair to slowly stretch and correct what nature hadn't formed correctly.

By the time I was thirteen years old, I had returned once more to the Shriners Hospital for Crippled Children to see the man who had done most of those surgeries, Dr. Dayton Riddle. This appointment was different. He sat me down and gently told me, "James, you're becoming a teenager now. We've done all we can surgically to correct your feet. But I'd like to talk to you about plastic surgery to reduce some of the scarring that's been left behind. That might be important as a teenager if you go to the pool or beach."

I didn't even need time to consider it. I asked, "Do I have to have it?"

He said, "No, not at all. This one would be cosmetic, just to remove some of the scars." And without hesitation, I told him I didn't want it.

I was tired of surgeries. Tired of being different. Tired of missing out on sports and activities because I was recovering when other kids were playing. But more than that, somewhere deep inside, I knew: Those scars told a story. They were reminders, not of brokenness but of how God had carried me through. I was never ashamed or embarrassed of those scars. I tell people that I could never be a foot model, but my feet are a roadmap of the grace and healing of a loving God. Those days in the hospital weren't awful, and I longed to go back every single time I was discharged, if you can imagine that. It might sound strange, but I loved being in the hospital. At home, there was chaos, abuse, neglect, instability, and fear. But at Shriners, there was routine, kindness, and comfort. A pastor came every Sunday and led services for the children. A volunteer we called "The Candy Man" came every Friday, passing out sweets from a shoebox with a smile.

I even attended public school there when my stays were long.

While most kids dreaded hospitals, I saw them as safe places—almost sacred ones. Looking back now, I realize God was there. He was providing me sanctuary in the middle of suffering. The scars on my feet don't represent disability or something undone. They represent divine protection. They're not reminders of what was wrong with me; they're reminders of what was right with God.

He knew what He was doing. He was preparing me for ministry long before I had a microphone or a message.

He was forming empathy, endurance, and dependence on Him.

He was teaching me how to love hurting people because I had been one. I didn't have a children's Bible or bedtime prayers. I didn't have Sunday School lessons. But I had something more basic and somehow more unshakable: I knew God was real. I knew He was listening when I talked to Him. I knew He loved me, even when I didn't feel lovable. And I knew He was going to protect me, no matter what.

That's why when I finally read the words of Jesus in Hebrews 13:5, "Never will I leave you; never will I forsake you," I didn't question it. I had already lived it. But in seminary years later, I learned something else about that verse that gave me even greater assurance and healing from the scars of my younger self. In the Greek, that statement is given using double negatives, really quadruple negatives. I'm glad Jesus didn't worry about using proper grammar! The original translation is, "I'll never, no, never, not ever leave you or forsake you!" It's called an "emphatic negation."[1] Jesus wanted to emphatically communicate His great and deep love for us. His love is so great that nothing could cause Him to leave or forsake me! Don't you love that?

That same truth became the foundation for my desire to walk with pastors, to mentor them, and to remind them that even the scars carry glory. That what we thought disqualified us may have actually been God's way of setting us apart. The present pastor doesn't lead from perfection; he or she leads from the places where God's grace has held them together. Some scars are sacred. And some wounds are really doors.

What if the scars on your life aren't signs of weakness but signs of God's hand?

REFLECTION FOR THE PASTOR'S HEART:

Where has God protected you in a way that didn't feel like protection at the time?

What would it take to thank God not just for the healing but for the wound that led you to Him? Can you thank Him now?

---

1. H.E. Dana and Julius R. Mantey, *A Manual Grammar of the Greek New Testament*, (NY: Macmillan Company, 1927), p. 266.

**Jesus is the model.
He led with compassion.
He touched the untouchable.
He limped to the cross and carried our wounds.
You are not less of a pastor because of your past.
You are more equipped to shepherd because of it.**

A STILL, SMALL VOICE

Pain insists upon being attended to. God whispers to us in our pleasures, speaks in our conscience, but shouts in our pain: it is His megaphone to rouse a deaf world.

–C.S. Lewis

All my life, I've known deep down that there was something more beyond what I could see. Some people might call that mystical, supernatural, or even spooky. But if you've ever felt it, you know exactly what I mean. It's the "knowingness" that there's something beyond this life and that somehow, you were made for it.

Even as a child, that awareness was there. I didn't have words for it. I didn't have theology to explain it. But I had that sacred whisper inside, like the Holy Spirit gently nudging me toward something, even in the chaos of my home, the instability of our life, and the pain of my physical condition.

Now, as a pastor and mentor, I often tell young leaders: The call doesn't always come in thunder. Sometimes, it comes in the calm before the storm.

I grew up in noise—not just the external kind but the internal dissonance of a life constantly being shaken. And yet, amid the shouting and chaos and uncertainty, there was a quiet thread: God's voice, present even when I didn't fully know Him yet.

Looking back, I see it clearly. There was a pull, a divine thread weaving its way through my earliest years. Though I didn't understand it then, I now believe that the Spirit speaks to every heart, and we either say yes, say no, or try to ignore Him.

But the call doesn't go away. Not when it's real. Not when it's from God.

Even before I ever stood behind a pulpit, I had the sense that my life had weight, not just from my trauma but from purpose. And I believe many pastors feel this same thing: a tug that starts early, even in the middle of mess.

I didn't grow up in the ideal conditions for ministry. Far from it. My home life was unstable. I was often alone. I was always recovering from surgery or navigating dysfunction and abuse. But in the silence of being a latchkey kid, the Holy Spirit found room to speak.

I spent a lot of time watching TV. It became my world. My escape. My rhythm. I memorized every TV show theme song, every jingle, "Plop, plop, fizz, fizz, oh what a relief it is"[1] or "My bologna has a first name, it's O-S-C-A-R…."[2] I could sing them on cue. Even then, I was learning how to communicate, how rhythm, language, and emotion could move people. I just didn't realize God was using commercial jingles to prepare a preacher!

I've often laughed at that thought: God can use anything, even commercials, to shape a communicator. We are all called. Every one of us. Ministry is not reserved for the platform. It's the work of the Kingdom, lived out daily in homes, in conversations, in kindness. But there is a unique, vocational calling, one where God says, "I want you to shepherd my people."

---

1. Alka-Seltzer. "Plop Plop, Fizz Fizz – Oh What a Relief It Is." Television commercial, 1976. YouTube, uploaded by The Museum of Classic Chicago Television, 27 Apr. 2023, www.youtube.com/watch?v=5nyMpaq8TJ0. Accessed 6 Nov. 2025.

2. Oscar Mayer. "My Bologna Has a First Name, It's O-S-C-A-R…" Television commercial, 1974. YouTube, uploaded by TSG Ch 2, 10 June 2017, www.youtube.com/watch?v=xRKTXCRqRXQ. Accessed 6 Nov. 2025.

And yet, that calling is not always clear at first. Sometimes, we feel it as restlessness. Sometimes, it's a moment of brokenness. Other times, it's a whisper that returns again and again.

Though church was not a part of my life at all in my youngest years, God still made sure I was exposed to the spirit realm. As I said, television was my friend and guardian for most of my childhood. I struggled from a young age with insecurities because of the condition of my feet. On Saturday mornings, before cartoons would begin rolling on all three of the channels we had back then, a young preacher named Oral Roberts would preach a thirty-minute sermon, and I sat and listened. At the end of every program, the televangelist would hold his hand up in front of the camera and ask the viewer to place their hand on the television screen over his, and he promised, with enough faith, God was going to heal the person watching.

My eight-year-old mind believed it with all of my heart. I'd place my hand on the screen each week, and I just *knew* God was going to heal my very deformed feet. After the prayer, I'd look down, and they looked the same. Though I was disappointed, I did it every week. I couldn't understand why God wouldn't heal me. As I got older and better understood the things of God, I realized that God *did* in fact answer the prayers of that little eight-year-old boy. The healing came through doctors, leg braces, plaster casts, and many surgeries, but today I can walk, run, and do just about anything anyone else can do. God heard my prayer and was preparing me to answer that same hope as a proclaimer of the Word.

Even though I didn't have language for it then, I can now say with confidence: I was called. Set apart. Even as life tried to pull me away, God kept re-centering me. I often think about and wonder about all the truly called men and women who won't say yes because they feel they are not qualified or have experienced things in life that have shattered their confidence that God could ever use them. I wonder about all the people who could have been reached for Christ, all the lives that could have been transformed, all the vessels of the Holy Spirit that fizzled out because the enemy holds our past over our heads. I stepped into pastoral ministry believing that if I worked hard enough, prayed long enough, and loved deeply enough, things would go smoothly.

They didn't.

Now, I must say I'm thankful because my good stories outnumber the tough ones. I've been blessed to be able to pastor some wonderful, godly people. But the difficult scenarios were enough to knock the wind out of me at times. I can honestly say I wasn't prepared for those. Or was I? It took a lot of prayer and counseling for me to finally see that the difficult circumstances, the pain as C.S. Lewis states, did prepare me in some ways. But ministry, I learned, is messy. There's a myth that floats around Christian leadership, an unspoken belief that if you're called, it will be easy. That you'll move from success to success, gaining favor like Joseph did in Potiphar's house. That your calling will be so clear and your gifts so evident, that people will follow without question.

That's not how it went for me.

After seminary, I started serving churches, small at first, then medium-sized, and eventually larger congregations. I did what I knew: I preached with passion, visited hospitals, mentored young leaders, wrote articles, led Bible studies, and poured myself into the people God gave me.

And there were beautiful results, baptisms, conversions, healing moments, and marriages restored. It was the real thing. But under the surface, something began to erode.

I didn't notice it at first. But looking back, I can see it so clearly now: I was building a version of myself that looked like "Pastor James" but didn't fully reflect the James who God had called and loved.

There's a weight to leadership that doesn't show up in the job description.

You're not just preaching a sermon; you're being watched at the grocery store. You're not just visiting a sick member; you're representing "the church" to the entire family. You're not just leading staff meetings; you're bearing the hopes, expectations, disappointments, and un-healed wounds of hundreds of people, who assume you'll never crack.

Somewhere along the way, I let those expectations shape me more than God's calling did.

I still prayed. Still read Scripture. Still loved Jesus. But I started performing.

I became the kind of pastor who stayed up all night tweaking ser-mon slides, not because they needed tweaking but because I couldn't handle disappointing the one person who might email the next day with a critique. I became the kind of pastor who smiled through grief, nodded through exhaustion, and preached sermons that lit others on fire while I quietly burned out inside.

I loved the people, but I feared losing their approval. That was my wilderness.

It's in moments like these that I think about Caleb.

Caleb was a spy sent into the Promised Land with Joshua. The other spies came back afraid, but Caleb stood firm. "We should go up and take possession of the land," he said, "for we can certainly do it" (Numbers 13:30).

What set Caleb apart wasn't strategy or charisma. It was his spirit. Scripture says he "has a different spirit" and "follows [the Lord] whole-heartedly" (Numbers 14:24). Caleb's strength wasn't in his muscles; it was in his devotion.

I think we need more Calebs in ministry. People who aren't shaped by fear, comparison, or applause but by wholehearted obedience to God. I long to be that kind of pastor.

One of the most transformative moments in my journey came during a staff meeting.

It wasn't dramatic. No one yelled. No one walked out. But a trusted staff member pulled me aside afterward and asked, "Do you know how exhausting it is to work for someone who never seems tired?"

At first, I bristled. And honestly at the same time, I took pride in it. I thought I was being strong for the team.

But what they saw was performance. And it made them feel like they couldn't be human either.

That conversation changed me. I started being honest about my fatigue. I admitted when I didn't have the answers. I started scheduling rest, not just time off but soul-restoring moments with God. I invited others to do the same.

And you know what happened?

Nothing fell apart. In fact, we grew closer. Ministry got richer. Trust deepened. People leaned in more, not less.

Biblical leadership isn't about image management, it's about surrender.

Jesus didn't come to be served but to serve (Matthew 20:28). And He didn't build His ministry on control, charisma, or credentials. He built it on intimacy with the Father.

He slipped away to pray. He wept at Lazarus' tomb. He cooked breakfast for His disciples after they abandoned Him. He didn't lead from a stage; He led from His knees.

If that's our model, why are we trying so hard to impress?

I had to learn to let go of being impressive.

That meant more vulnerability from the pulpit. More "I don't know" in counseling sessions. More laughter with my family. More weeping with my staff. It meant learning to live with what St. Augustine called "rightly ordered love:" loving God first, others second, and myself rightly in the process.[3] When I lead from that place, I find freedom. Not perfection. Not applause. But freedom.

And that's what I want for you, too.

Pastor, Christian Leader, if you've ever wondered, Am I really called? I understand.

If your life didn't come wrapped in a neat little box labeled "ministry material."

---

3. St. Augustine. *City of God.* Translated by Henry Bettenson, Penguin Classics, 1984; originally Book XV, Chapter 22.

If you've ever thought God could never use someone with your history.

If you've been waiting for a "burning bush" moment, but all you've had is a quiet tug.

Let this chapter be your confirmation.

God does not always call with claps of thunder.

Sometimes, He calls with the still, small voice that keeps showing up, even in cartoons, commercials, and chaos.

REFLECTION FOR THE PASTOR'S HEART:

When did you first feel the tug of something more—even if you didn't yet call it "ministry"?

Have you dismissed or downplayed your calling because it didn't come dramatically? Why or why not?

What "ordinary" experiences might God have used to prepare you to speak with boldness and empathy?

**The present pastor doesn't always arrive
with credentials.**

**Sometimes, he or she arrives with questions and
a whisper in their spirit that won't go away.**

DIVINE CONNECTIONS

*God never said that the journey would be easy, but He did say
that the arrival would be worthwhile.*

—Max Lucado

Soon after I graduated with a college degree in communications, I married the love of my life, Natalie. We started out as many young couples do, excited about the future, moving toward our careers, and longing to start a family. We couldn't have come from two more different backgrounds. It was eerily similar to my parents. Of course, my experience was abusive, unstable, and chaotic. She was born and grew up in the same house her entire life and had two wonderful, stable parents and a childhood full of love and care. I wanted everything she had, and I set out to break cycles and live that settled life I'd longed for my entire life. I stepped into a dream career in advertising, bought a great house, and tackled the world. But I was unsettled and didn't quite know why. I had gotten serious about my faith and church in my college years and had this gnawing feeling that I might be called to ministry. I had no framework for that, and I was sure someone with my background could never lead people to Jesus. I wanted to serve God but only on the sidelines. Money was my goal. And preachers were poor! I'd had enough of that.

I thought ministry would solve the ache I'd carried for years. I thought finally saying yes to my call would lift the uneasiness I'd wrestled with since my teens. For a while, it did. But calling always comes with cost, and I was just starting to learn how deep that cost would run.

Let me go back a bit.

In the early 1990s, when Natalie and I were still living in South Carolina, we decided to help plant a new United Methodist Church in Spartanburg. The lead pastor was a 57-year-old woman named Mary Rowell. And to this day, I can say without hesitation, she was the best preacher I've ever heard. Period.

Mary didn't just preach. She burned with the fire of God. She knew the Scriptures backwards and forwards, but more than that, she knew how to bring them to life. Mary was every bit of 6'2" and always dressed to the nines, her big, coiffed head of red hair always in place.

She had a zeal for Jesus that extended far beyond that little pulpit in an old real estate office and into the community. And we were drawn to that.

Natalie and I were in our early twenties at the time, young and idealistic, and we thought maybe if we just got close to something like this, something fresh, something alive, it would satisfy that deep, gnawing desire I had to serve in full-time ministry without actually stepping into it.

The truth? I was scared.

I didn't want to go into ministry, not only because of limited salaries but because I didn't think pastors had creative or fulfilled lives. They had to sacrifice everything and scrounge to pay their bills. I had grown up watching my family struggle for every dime and quarter. I knew what it was like to count out coins for gas and live paycheck to paycheck, steal packs of condiments from restaurants, stand in line to receive government cheese (which is why I still love Velveeta), and swipe toilet paper from public restrooms. I wanted more for my life and for my future family.

So, I chose advertising. I chose stability.

But stability has a cost too, especially when God keeps tapping you on the shoulder.

I thought helping plant a church would scratch the itch. It didn't.

Then one day, out of the blue, Pastor Mary called and asked to meet me for lunch. We were still worshiping in a makeshift real estate office and had begun dreaming about a building campaign. I assumed she wanted to talk strategy. I had just become lay leader of the church.

We met, ate, and talked about life, ministry, and God's faithfulness. But not once did she bring up the church. Then, just as we were standing to leave, she looked me dead in the eye and said: "James, everyone seems to know you're called to full-time ministry except you. What are you going to do about it?" Then, she was just quiet.

I stood there like a deer in headlights, stunned. It's a rare occasion that I'm at a loss for words, but I couldn't speak. I had never spoken with her about my call. Barely anyone knew, except Natalie, and she was not at all thrilled with the idea. She didn't marry a preacher. I wasn't sure she ever wanted to be a preacher's wife.

But that lunch? It cracked something open in me.

I walked back into my office that day, picked up the phone, and called Natalie.

"You're not going to believe what Mary just said to me."

Within six months, our house was sold, I had applied to seminary, and we were preparing to move. At the time, I had decided on Duke Divinity School. It was a respected United Methodist seminary, and I felt it was the right choice. But a few months before we were set to move, my brother-in-law Charles, one of the smartest, strongest Christians I knew, suggested I look into another school—one I'd never even heard of.

"Asbury Theological Seminary in Kentucky," he said. "Maxie Dunnam is the new president, and I think you ought to check it out."

I didn't know anything about Kentucky except for good basketball and Abraham Lincoln. But I was curious, especially because I had just finished leading a Bible study at our new church, *The Workbook of Living Prayer*, a book written by Maxie Dunnam himself.

The book had changed the way I prayed, and it had changed others too. I remember thinking maybe this was God rolling out the red carpet.

So, I called Asbury and scheduled a visit. As soon as I stepped on campus, something felt right—more right than anything I'd ever experienced. The peace was unmistakable. I knew I had to bring Natalie back to see it.

We made another trip. The feeling remained. So, we changed course and committed to Kentucky.

During one of those visits, I met Lindsey Davis, who was at the time, the district superintendent in Lexington. Lindsey had left a career at the University of Kentucky to pursue ministry, so he understood my leap from the business world. He told me that if I came to Asbury, he was confident he could place me in a local church as a student pastor.

That made everything real. This wasn't just school. This was a calling. A life. A new identity.

I was going to be a pastor!

We moved. We found a rental home. We settled into a modest rhythm. And right before our move five hours away from family, we received the miraculous news that Natalie was pregnant with our son, John.

God was already showing us that His ways are not our ways.

But then came the biggest surprise of all. At a Christian conference in Lake Junaluska, North Carolina, just before our move, I met up with two Kentucky preachers, Quentin Scholtz and his friend, Mike Powers. We talked for about forty minutes, and somewhere in that conversation I shared my struggles about going into full-time ministry and my uncertainty about what seminary to attend. It was like I'd known them my whole life. I couldn't believe it.

I had even seen Mike's picture in an Asbury Seminary ad just weeks before.

Before we parted ways, Quentin said something I'll never forget. And he's the kind of guy you must listen to when he speaks. If you don't, he'll say it again. And louder! This guy had Jesus flowing out of his spirit. He grabbed my arm, looked me in the eye and said,

"Hey James, I graduated from Duke. But if I had it to do over again, I'd go to Asbury."

That was the final confirmation I needed.

I visited Kentucky one more time and stayed in Quentin's home. He showed me around, answered my questions, and became one of my dear friends. God kept placing these divine connections in my path.

I had been running from my calling for years. But in that season, God didn't just whisper. He shouted. He lined everything up. And finally, I said yes.

I didn't know then how costly and beautiful that "yes" would be.

But I knew I was in.

REFLECTION FOR THE PASTOR'S HEART:

What doubts have you struggled with as you've pursued your calling?

What confirmations of your calling have you experienced along the way?

Take a moment and pray a prayer of thanksgiving and gratitude for those divine connections and those who confirmed your calling.

THE WEIGHT OF THE COLLAR

Do not neglect the gift you have, which was given you by prophecy when the council of elders laid their hands on you. Practice these things, immerse yourself in them, so that all may see your progress.

—1 Timothy 4:14–15 ESV

There's a cartoon I saw in a ministry magazine years ago. A pastor is standing in the doorway of his office, listening to a parishioner pour out her financial troubles. She's anxious. Desperate. Needing help. What she doesn't see, just beyond the open door, is a shelf behind the pastor piled with his own overdue bills, unopened envelopes, and red-stamped late notices.

That image stuck with me. Because that's how it feels.

You carry the weight of the whole room while quietly breaking in your own.

Over the years, people have said to me, "I don't know how you do it, Pastor. I could never have your job." And I usually smile and say, "It's not an easy job, but the blessings outweigh the hard stuff." And I mean it. I really do.

But that doesn't mean the weight isn't real and heavy. I was in the United Methodist system for the first twenty-eight years of my ministry. I loved it and learned so much. But only because I dug for more. The system itself often handcuffed me and held me back from leading in the ways I really wanted to lead. I was always afraid one misstep would have me removed from my church and sent to some remote area as punishment. It never happened to me. But it did happen to some of my colleagues. I noticed that pastors who were much better preachers than I, who often had "better" pastor's hearts than I had were stuck in places where they couldn't flourish because they either refused to "play the game" or had disappointed a parishioner, district superintendent, or worse—a bishop. I began to notice that most of us who moved up the Methodist ladder of success had learned to navigate a sick system.

I learned to do that. I'm not proud of it. God was gracious enough to allow me to accomplish some good things for His glory in spite of it. But I knew this wasn't God's best for us. I always had integrity, but I compromised and overlooked some unhealthy dynamics in order to hit my goals and stay on the path to being seen as a good, successful, professional pastor and what I believed was God's vision for my ministry.

My first full-time appointment was to a fairly new congregation that had been started by a fiery conference evangelist. They received a patch of over thirty acres and an old horse barn and planted a church. I was the third pastor in five years, which should have been my first red flag. My heart was full. I was ready to change the world for Jesus and dared anyone to get in my way. I slept, ate, and breathed church. Natalie was the glue that held everything together because I was much too busy doing the Lord's work. Insert winking emoji here!

No doubt, I honestly wanted to see spiritual growth and fruit. I continued to grow in leadership. I saw changed lives. I baptized new believers. I watched young families come alive in their faith.

The church grew. The vision expanded. We launched a building campaign and completed the facility. I stayed through its dedication and then, a year later, accepted an appointment to a well-known congregation outside Lexington, Kentucky. It was a new chapter, and I walked into it with joy, but I left behind people I deeply loved.

At this new assignment, God was clearly moving. We launched a second campus. We saw lives changed, hearts opened, and people healed. There was real, visible fruit.

But with that fruit came pressure.

This church had a strong presence of business professionals who were used to success, strategy, and structure. And because I had come from that world, I knew how to speak their language. I also knew the unspoken expectations I would be stepping into:

Be excellent

Be competent

Be strong

Be visionary

Be bulletproof

And here's the truth: I was moving in the Spirit. Most days, I was prayed up, rooted, obedient, and aligned with God. I journaled regularly. I cried out for God to keep me healthy and real. I had mentors and accountability in my life.

But the American model of pastoring, the polished, always smiling, always strategic, always winning pastor, was still chasing me.

And sometimes...well, almost always, I chased it back.

I had been pastoring for a few years when I first realized that the pulpit wasn't enough.

Preaching had always been my passion. There's something electric about opening the Word of God, praying over a text, and delivering it to a room full of people whose hearts and lives you love. It's sacred. It's exhilarating. It's terrifying. And, honestly, it had become my safety net.

I knew how to preach. I could do it with skill and conviction. But somewhere along the line, I started hiding behind the pulpit. It was safer there than in the quiet moments after the benediction, moments when someone would grab my arm and say, "Can I talk to you about something real?"

Ministry isn't just a Sunday task. It's an everyday invitation to walk with people in their pain and let them walk with you in yours. The former, I did with consistency and, frankly, excellence. The latter, I failed miserably, allowing no one to see my difficulties and struggles.

I was at a church that had "great potential" when the veil started to tear for me. We were in the middle of launching a second campus. There were skeptical people telling me it couldn't be done in the context and culture we were in and that made me want to do it even more. So, I worked, prayed, and sermonized day and night to prove the naysayers wrong. The sermons were hitting. Attendance was rising. New families were coming. From the outside, everything looked great.

We started a second service targeting the unchurched in a local movie theater. I reached back to my old advertising days and came up with what would be a very successful tagline: "No Suit, No Tie, No Problem!" Our church budget began to grow, and we spent every extra dime on marketing, advertising, mass mailings, new equipment, and smoke machines. I recruited a young pastor who wore jeans and a t-shirt each Sunday to help me lead worship. We offered a food bank, free haircuts for kids, and had community events where we gave away new tv sets, movie tickets, and PlayStations.

We had to face police interventions because we caused traffic issues at our events. The local McDonald's complained because we blocked their entrance, so I negotiated buying gift certificates with the manager to give away at our community events. People came to our services, hearts were changed, and many found they felt welcome in a church, some for the first time in their lives. The same district superintendent who had questioned my wisdom in starting the second campus later called me to ask if he could help me by sending a "campus pastor" to assist me in managing the growth. It was glorious.

But inside, I was unraveling.

I had convinced myself that as long as I was achieving externally, I didn't need to worry too much about what was happening internally. I wasn't ignoring God, but I was functioning in my own strength. The Holy Spirit became more of a silent partner than the lead voice. And I could tell even though no one else could.

It showed up in subtle ways. I was less patient with staff. I was emotionally absent at home. My prayer life shrunk from deep conversations to quick bullet points. I still prayed, but it felt like checking a box more than meeting with a friend. I slowly allowed Natalie to take the main lead in raising our children. I immersed myself in being the perfect, professional pastor. Nothing could get in the way, and I justified it by convincing myself that I was the only hope for people not to end up in hell. It's a crazy paradox. I created my own hell in order to keep people out of theirs. That's what model pastors do, right?

Addiction has haunted my family for generations. My mother, who had died in a drunk driving crash years earlier, had struggled deeply with addiction. My younger sister, six years my junior, had walked a similar road. And no matter how much I loved her or how often we talked, I couldn't pull her out.

One Sunday morning, just ten minutes before I was scheduled to walk into the sanctuary and preach, a knock came on my office door. A parishioner said, "There's a phone call for you. It's from a family member."

I hesitated. "Can it wait?"

She looked at me grimly. "I think it's important."

I stepped over to the phone and picked up the line. My aunt's voice came through from South Carolina.

"Jamie… your sister overdosed. She passed away last night."

Time stopped. I don't remember what I said next. I only remember that moment the gut-punch I felt, the flashbacks to childhood, and the sinking sense that the past had never really left me, no matter how fast I ran away from it.

I had given news like that to people too many times to count. I truly loved people, and it was important to me to be sensitive, supportive, and compassionate in those times. I never would have allowed someone to "go back to work" minutes after receiving that kind of information. My world had just flipped upside down. My little sister was gone. An overdose. The final chapter of a battle I had prayed for years would end differently.

I stood in that office with the phone pressed so hard to my ear it hurt because I wanted to be sure no one heard what was being said on the other end. It was a room where I had written hundreds of sermons, sat with and comforted so many distraught parishioners, a place of prayer, a place of refuge, safety, and hope. It suddenly transformed into a room of shame and condemnation where all I could hear was the rattling of the old water-filled heater behind me.

I stood in that old, beautiful building with the architecture patterned after the Winchester Cathedral in England, where I was so proud to be their pastor. It was filled with God's people, and yet I felt totally alone and so, so ashamed. I was a pastor, and I couldn't help my own sister. Who was I kidding? I felt like an imposter. All of the holiness I had connected to that room seemed to fade. My hands went numb. My stomach turned. It was the first and only time I ever felt like I was having a panic attack. My heart pounded in a rhythm that didn't match the ticking of the clock counting down to the start of worship. I had to stop the tears. I couldn't grieve, not yet. The shock froze everything inside me. My mind spun with disbelief: How do I go from this phone call to a pulpit?

I put down the phone, wiped my face, then opened my drawer and took out a bottle of Visine. I put two drops in each eye, took the green stole off the rack behind my office door, and placed it around my neck and over my robe. The theology behind both were not lost on me even in that moment. The robe I wore because as I proclaimed the Word of God nothing should be seen that would distract my parishioners from that message. The green stole around my neck represented the towel that Jesus used to wash his disciples' feet—servanthood. I straightened my notes, placed them in my Bible, and walked out as if nothing had happened. People came in the side door for worship, leaving their Sunday School classes, laughing, talking, being the church and community, greeting me as I walked by—"Good morning, Pastor James! I'll see you tonight at Bible Study!" I smiled. My body moved, but my spirit was somewhere else, somewhere between earth and heaven, between heartbreak and obedience.

And then, I preached.

We had baptisms that morning. We were recognizing a large group of youth just back from a mission trip. The sanctuary was full. The church had more than doubled in attendance in just a few years. The bulletin was printed. The people were smiling.

And I… was broken. But no one would've ever, ever known.

I stood up. I delivered the sermon. I led the celebrations. I gave the benediction. I told no one.

Then, I walked out the back door and texted Natalie. I still can't believe I did that. Texting, I told her about the call. I spoke to no one, got in my car, and drove home alone.

I didn't want to be surrounded. I didn't want comfort. I didn't want anyone to see me not be okay. Because I had learned, even if silently: The exemplary pastor doesn't fall apart in public. I was "Rev. Williams:" a respected community leader, who, just two weeks before, had opened the state legislature with prayer at the Kentucky General Assembly in Frankfort; a member of the Chamber of Commerce board; and a Rotarian. I was on television each week and on the local radio station almost every day. I wrote a monthly column in the city's newspaper. That guy needed to preach and lead in those moments. But the physician needed medicine. My pride took over once again. I was embarrassed and angry. And I knew I had to deal with it. Alone.

I got home, sat in silence, and asked myself:

"James, what are you doing? These people love you. They would hold you. They would pray for you. But instead, you gave them a smile and a sermon."

I wanted to be strong. I wanted to appear unshaken. I wanted to be "the one with answers."

But inside, I was asking the biggest questions of my life.

A few minutes later, my sixteen-year-old son, John, walked in. He had driven separately to church that day, but his mom told him about the phone call I'd received. He ran up the stairs, burst through my bedroom door, weeping, and threw his arms around me.

"I'm so sorry, Dad. I'm so, so sorry."

At that moment, that hug began to heal something deep in me.

John had always been sensitive. And smart. And kind. But I hadn't expected him to be the one who would hold me together. God used him that day. God showed me through my son what I hadn't let myself see through so many others: I was human. I was hurting. I needed healing too.

I had believed the lie that my pain had no place in the pulpit.

That's not biblical.

Jesus wept. David wrote psalms in anguish. Isaiah was the "weeping prophet." Paul preached while chained in prison. Elijah begged God to let him die, and God met him there with rest and a whisper.

I was so very prideful. Was I better and stronger than these men of great faith? Real pastoring means never let them see you sweat! Right? Wrong.

Real leadership isn't about being unshakable. It's about being honest enough to need God in front of your people.

I realized that I had been more concerned with being a strong leader than with being a present father or even dedicated to my own self-care. And now, here was my son showing up with the kind of empathy and grace I didn't even know if he had seen modeled by me.

That hug healed something.

I think of Joseph often, betrayed by his brothers, falsely accused, left in a prison, forgotten. But every time he's described in Genesis, the text says, "The LORD was with Joseph" (Genesis 39:2, 21, 23).

Not because Joseph was always strong but because Joseph was always surrendered.

When Pharaoh finally summoned him and asked him to interpret a dream, Joseph said, "I cannot do it…but God will give Pharaoh the answer he desires" (Genesis 41:16).

That's biblical leadership. Not, "I've got this," but "God has this, and I'm listening."

In my ministry, I've had to learn that honesty is more powerful than polish. That people don't want a perfect pastor; they want a present one.

And when I started being present, things changed.

I started showing up for people, not with answers but with presence. I listened more. I interrupted less. I cried more easily. I preached with more rawness. I started telling the truth, not just theological truth but emotional truth.

My preaching became better too, not because I added more points but because I stopped hiding.

And something beautiful began to happen in my ministry. People opened up. They started telling their own stories about addiction, loss, regret, and reconciliation. They leaned in when I talked about grace because they knew I needed it too.

Ministry became a place of healing, not just a place of hustle.

I learned that being a "model pastor" isn't about looking like a model. It's about modeling what it means to trust God with your actual life, not the version you think people want.

That's when I began to realize I couldn't keep living behind the costume. I couldn't keep being the model pastor. It wasn't working. It wasn't sustainable. And it wasn't honest.

The church had loved me. But I needed to learn how to love myself again as a man, as a father, and as a servant of Christ.

In the years to come, I would sit in counseling with a woman named Bonnie Crandall, sharp, kind, and brutally honest. She helped me see that I had sacrificed my family on the altar of ministry. Not out of malice. Out of imbalance.

I learned that my family had borne the weight of my unhealed past. I was determined that the model pastor had to have a model family. The unhealed places in my heart could stay that way without the pain of peeling them back to heal if they could support my ministry by performing as well. None of this was ever expressed explicitly but ministry families can easily fall into the category of supporting the pastor's unrealistic expectations for the sake of giving the congregation assurance that their clergy leader "has it all together." The same unconditional love that had been given by Christ to me so freely would be seemingly withheld (however unintentional) from my children until they could "get it right." Even though their father couldn't remotely get it right at times. Celebrating my children's strengths had at times given way to protecting my ministry. These were not God's but *my* expectations. My children were kind, sensitive, brilliant, and had a wonderful sense of humor. My performance issues at times communicated that wasn't enough. I needed them to help me present my strong front and do nothing to make me look like anything other than the perfect father. Oh, yes. I took very seriously 1 Timothy 3:4 (NASB) where the Apostle Paul said, a pastor *"must be* one who manages his own household well, keeping his children under control with all dignity"* (italics mine for emphasis). The problem was I often didn't hold myself to the same standards to which I was holding my children. My role was sometimes more important than my calling. I had to come to terms with the fact that I wasn't just called to pastor. I was called to be a gentle guide to my family with integrity. I wanted to do this in my heart of hearts but constantly looked over my shoulder to be sure no one saw the clergy collar slipping, even if it meant keeping my family tethered to the same unhealthy expectations that I lived with daily. In spite of my inner struggles, my children have become accomplished, well-adjusted adults. I was loving and attentive, but if I had a do over, I'd allow them to be much freer without such unfair expectations. I would have been much more present with not just my congregation but with two of my greatest blessings, my children. (Psalm 127:3). One of the most poignant moments in processing all of this with Bonnie was when she very directly said to me, "James, you need to nurture the relationships with those who will be standing around your deathbed." Pastor, Christian leader, protect your children and allow them to exist outside of your work. They didn't ask to live in a fishbowl. Hold your greatest blessings gently.

Through counseling, I learned Natalie had stood in the gap more times than I could count. A growing church, evening meetings, leadership conferences, and community accolades like speaking to schools, civic clubs, and other high-profile events took every extra moment. My loving and supportive wife became my assistant to helping me achieve, while she, in some ways, became a single mother. After all, I was doing God's work.

So often pastors have shied away from counseling, but I must tell you that the worst mistake I ever made was believing the lie that a truly called person would never need the assistance of a counselor. Never believe that's a sign of failure. In order to be a stronger and healthier husband and father, I needed an objective person, unimpressed with my achievements, to hold my feet to the fire. Having the accountability of sitting in a room being honest about who I really was helped me to finally see that being a "successful" pastor meant nothing if it came at the cost of being a non-present father and an inattentive husband.

I sat across from Bonnie and unloaded years of unspoken wounds. Ministry had cost me, and I hadn't counted the price. The first several sessions, she just listened to me vent. I'd served on some denominational boards with her, and she had only encountered the "all together James," and I was horrified to be honest with her. I thought if I was too honest, she'd blow my cover. Maybe I needed to go a few states over and get a counselor where no one knew me. But I decided to chance it.

I started with my old mainstay of giving as much surface information as I could without revealing anything real. I was in the midst of this one session, and in the middle of it, Bonnie interrupted me. "James, James, James. Listen, my friend, you need to understand something. My father was a pastor, my husband was a pastor, two of my brothers-in-law were clergy (all Methodist), and I have worked on church staffs for over 25 years. If you think I can't see through BS, you have another thing coming. Now, we'll do this authentically or not at all. You'd be wasting your money and my time."

I sat there like a deer in headlights. And in typical Bonnie fashion, she picked up a toy magic wand that played mystical tunes as she waved it through the air and waved it all around my head each time I started on a dishonest rant. She'd wave the wand to show me how ridiculous I sounded. It sounds completely crazy, but it changed my life.

After I'd been with Bonnie for some time, from moments of laughing hysterically to almost being crumpled on her office floor in terrible emotional pain, she looked at me and said, "I think you've finally realized you're a COGPOW." A what? I thought. "James, You're a Child Of God and Person Of Worth. That's all that really matters."[1]

It was one of those moments that I'll never forget. My version of a super pastor worthy of my own comic book series only considered performance and success. Being the well put-together community leader with an "S" on my chest was the unspoken goal. But I was discovering that God wanted my warts as well as my gifts.

Bonnie helped me see that my desire to be strong for others had kept me from being known. She also helped me recognize the ways I had hurt my own family.

I had put my calling above my kids. I had missed dinners, homework sessions, school projects, and other events all in the name of ministry. And though I never intended to neglect them, I had.

John and Mary Grace had both lived in a fishbowl. They had been expected to behave, perform, and reflect well on me. They had to not only figure out who they were in Christ but at the same time, live with the weight of my image.

Natalie, too, had felt the heaviness of my image and borne it. With grace, yes. But also, in silence. She loved people deeply. She understood the call. She is an extremely genuine and empathetic person. But she had spent too many nights alone, while I poured myself out for others.

It was time to re-center. To remember the call wasn't to be the savior of the church. That job had already been filled.

I began spending more time in Scripture, not for sermon prep but for survival.

---

1. For a deeper look at what it means to be a COGPOW, see *Confronting the Thief Within* by Wes Olds and Bonnie Crandall, *(Invite Press, 2023)*.

I read Joseph's story again, this time noticing the quiet resilience of his suffering. Betrayed, imprisoned, forgotten—but never abandoned. "You intended to harm me," Joseph said to his brothers, "God intended it for good" (Genesis 50:20). That verse became my anchor.

I revisited Caleb's story. At 85 years old, he said, "Give me this mountain" (Joshua 14:12 KJV). His strength wasn't in his youth—it was in his faith. He believed God was still calling him forward.

And I lingered in the Psalms, in David's cries, confessions, and songs of surrender. The shepherd-king who messed up royally but kept coming back to God's heart.

What I learned in that season is something I hope every pastor takes to heart:

You are not the ministry. You are the minister.

Your value is not in your metrics. It's in your identity.

And your call is not to perfection. It's to presence.

I began to rebuild. Slowly. Honestly. Painfully. And God met me there. I wasn't wearing a title in that place. I wasn't leading a congregation. I was just a man on his knees, saying yes all over again.

Back in the 1980s, during my high school years, I worked as a lifeguard at a well-known ministry called Heritage USA. The PTL Club was growing quickly, and I became one of its 3,000 employees. I had no interest in God, but I was required to attend a Bible study in order to work there. That was my first encounter with prevenient grace. Even in a Pentecostal ministry rocked by scandal and excess, God used it to get to my heart. I became friends with a group of teenagers close to Jim and Tammy Bakker's daughter, Tammy Sue. Though her family was famous, Tammy Sue was just a regular teenager, who was kind and one of my co-workers. I found myself in rooms with her parents, and they were very kind to me and, I believe, knew my home life was difficult.

We were all typical teens and mainly made fun of all the hoopla at PTL. I had no interest in being a pious Christian. Years later, I met a friend of Jim Bakker's, and he told Jim he met me, and I had ended up a Methodist pastor. By then, Jim had served five years in federal prison for FCC violations and mail fraud, was released, had gone through a very public divorce, and Billy and Ruth Graham had given him a place to stay while he got back on his feet. He was now remarried and hosting a new religious TV show in Branson, Missouri. He reached out and asked if I could fly to Branson and be interviewed on his show. So, I went.

After the taping, we all went out to eat, and I rode with Jim in a car by ourselves. On the way, he looked at me with tears in his eyes and said, "Aren't you ashamed to be seen with me?"

I immediately said, "Jim, it's level at the foot of the cross. I have as many sins as you have. Mine just weren't plastered across newspapers all over the world."

I had with the rest of the world seen through the eyes of the media a crooked preacher who was, as Rev. Jerry Falwell described him, a "cancer on the Body of Christ." But that day I saw a broken man who lost everything because of ambition, lustful desires, and the American version of Christianity. It was a cathartic moment that hit me right between the eyes. In Jim's own way, he was saying, "learn from my mistakes." He and I have deep theological differences, but he stood face-to-face with his demons, and God restored him. That trip made me think long and hard about the remainder of my ministry. My son was almost grown, but I knew I wanted to show my daughter a healthier way to serve Jesus. I was learning something deeper about the call to ministry. Yes, it includes humility. Yes, it requires strong faith. Yes, it means showing people how to trust God in the storm.

But it does not mean pretending there is no storm.

There were days when I played the part of the confident shepherd while inside, I was a cracked jar. And sometimes, I felt that ache most intensely on Sunday mornings, just as I was about to proclaim a Word that I was myself struggling to live.

I always believed in God's goodness. I never doubted His love. But I wrestled hard with His timing. I wrestled with my need to succeed. With the weight of being "the guy." With the spiritual performance so many of us have learned to perfect.

I longed to be fully real behind the pulpit and behind closed doors.

And over time, I began to see something beautiful: The more I dropped the act, the more God showed up.

Hebrews 4:15 says:

> *"For we do not have a high priest who is unable to empathize with our weaknesses, but we have one who has been tempted in every way, just as we are—yet he did not sin."*

Jesus felt what we feel. The difference is, He didn't fake it.

He cried. He withdrew. He said, "My soul is overwhelmed with sorrow" (Mark 14:34).

He was misunderstood. Rejected. Pressed on every side.

Yet He never hid behind strength. And He never asked His followers to pretend.

Pastors don't need to be perfect. They need to be present—with God, their family, and their people.

REFLECTION FOR THE PASTOR'S HEART:

What would it look like for you to preach through your pain, giving yourself permission to share deeply?

What are two ways you could begin to allow God to minister through your honesty, not just your strength?

How can you start leading with transparency or with a version of yourself that allows others to follow your lead in living in freedom?

Where could you begin to drop your guard and let your people carry you, the way you've carried them?

The perfect pastor isn't one who never breaks.

They are the ones who know where to fall when they do.

PERFORMANCE

*The beginning of love is to let those we love be perfectly themselves,
and not to twist them to fit our own image.*

—*Thomas Merton*

Not growing up in the church was both a blessing and a curse for me. As I said earlier, my life was extremely nomadic. We moved from place to place most of my childhood, finally settling back in the city where I was born when I was around fourteen. That return gave me something I hadn't had before: consistency. Stability. The kind of grounding many kids take for granted.

I graduated from high school in that same city and eventually became the first person in my immediate family to go to college. But those teenage years were transformative for another reason because they brought me into closer relationship with my maternal grandmother and my paternal grandparents. Those connections, especially with my grandmother, shaped me in more ways than I understood at the time.

My grandmother was a strong woman. Faithful. Resilient. She didn't preach at me, but she made it clear that she believed in the Lord and that she believed in me. I didn't want to disappoint her. Her words were often simple, but they stuck: "Jamie, hold your head up, but keep God first." I didn't always know what that meant. But I knew she lived it.

She sacrificed a lot for me. Though I qualified for a good bit of financial aid, I still needed $800 for my freshman year. I had no idea how I was going to come up with that. Though I agonized over ever having to ask anyone for help, I was desperate and went to my grandmother and asked if she could co-sign a loan with me. I was embarrassed to even ask her, and I could tell she knew that. She said she would do it, but I couldn't tell anyone, especially not my grandfather. He was a hard, abusive man, and it would have been a disaster if he found out. I decided I would go to a bank an hour away so no one in my small town would know.

My grandmother and I walked into the bank together, and I felt like I was going to the principal's office. I was a kid with no resources, and she was a 60-year-old woman with little income and a job in a textile mill. I'll never forget the loan officer in the First Union bank in Charolotte, NC. She never should have given us that loan. After meeting for an hour, she left us in the office for about thirty minutes. I was scared but mainly didn't want my grandmother to be embarrassed. I finally looked at her and said, "Mema, let's go. I'll figure this out another way." Almost in that instant, the loan officer returned and said, "Mrs. Blackwell, I just need your signature, and we'll cut your grandson the check today." I couldn't believe it. We left the bank and got a milkshake!

This is an absolutely true story that I've told no one about until this writing.

So, when I enrolled in college, I threw myself into it, wanting her to be proud. But during my senior year, my grandmother was diagnosed with an aggressive brain cancer. It happened fast. The decline, the surgery, and the funeral all blurred together. She passed away just months before I graduated.

I was devastated. And I was angry. I had already begun my ascent up the mountain of achievement and success. I hit the ground running in college. I managed our campus radio station, became president of my fraternity, worked part-time for the Billy Graham Association at the ministry's radio station, and started a side business. I met Natalie and dating her meant I must go to church. No problem. I was there, at least physically, each week. I made enough money in my side business to buy an engagement ring, and I thought all of this was surely going to align me with God enough to answer my every prayer. Losing my grandmother, however, was a devastating blow.

Why would God take her before she got to see me walk that stage? Why would a woman who had already endured so much have to leave this earth so soon? I had more questions than I had faith. For a time, I wandered. Not physically. I kept going to class, kept showing up for work. But spiritually? I wandered.

And yet, even in my wandering, seeds were being planted.

I didn't know it then, but I was being prepared. God was building something in me that required sorrow and confusion—and silence.

I now believe every true servant-leader walks through fire. It's not optional. You don't get authority without adversity. You don't get wisdom without wounds.

The towel and the table. Those two sacred images of Jesus had started to mark my soul. The towel, which He used to wash feet. And the table, where He broke bread with the ones who would betray and deny Him.

Those are the real symbols of leadership. Not a microphone or a platform.

Over the years, I've learned that nothing forms you like pain. And nothing tests you like people. And nothing, absolutely nothing will test you like the people you love and shepherd. Nothing.

When you've been in ministry long enough, you learn to walk with a certain spiritual limp. The kind that reminds you of both where you've been and who brought you through it. I had more than a limp by the time I stepped into my role as a district superintendent. I carried spiritual bruises, some still fresh.

I never wanted to be a superintendent.

It's a prestigious role, sure, an administrative position over pastors and churches, often seen as a "promotion" in Methodist circles. But I didn't want it. Not really. I accepted the appointment out of obedience and a sense of responsibility. I was administratively gifted. I could lead meetings. I understood systems. I had learned skills of mediation.

But nothing about it felt like home to me.

And yet, it was one of the most important shaping seasons of my life.

As district superintendent of one of the largest districts in Kentucky, I oversaw 110 pastors and 102 congregations. My calendar was relentless. Conflict resolution, pastoral care, disciplinary hearings, charge conferences… I became a spiritual firefighter. The phone never stopped ringing.

But here's what they don't tell you: When you start supervising pastors, you have to confront the mirror of your own weaknesses.

There were days I sat across from pastors and had to correct them for the very things I struggled with myself: pride, workaholism, and insecurity masked as confidence. I found myself saying things like, "You need to spend more time with your family," knowing full well I had missed many hours with my own family. Or "You need a Sabbath rhythm," while reviewing and responding to emails on my day off.

I wasn't being dishonest. I just hadn't yet learned how to lead from the middle of my own sanctification. I was growing, but I hadn't arrived. And I felt the hypocrisy of trying to guide others from an unfinished place. Almost weekly, I would encounter some situation with a pastor or church leader going off the rails and saw myself in the same situations, either physically or internally. My dilemma wasn't that I had those struggles; it was that I was afraid to ask anyone to help me overcome them. I look back now and see that

I expended so much energy on trying to cover those things so others wouldn't know when I could have been honest and just said to an older pastor or mentor that I needed help.

A few years ago, a colleague of mine (who ironically, I supervised) said to me when I talked about those struggles, he couldn't believe "James Williams struggled with those things. You were the smooth guy we joked with one another about!"

I responded, "I'm so, so sorry you didn't know that about me. I apologize that I couldn't be more authentic and vulnerable." It was fear and pride that drove me in those things and not the Holy Spirit.

There's a time in the life of Joshua, long after he succeeds Moses, where he learns to lead without being Moses. He doesn't part seas, but he does part rivers. He doesn't confront Pharaoh, but he does face down fortified cities. Joshua learns to lead as Joshua and not as a replica of the man before him. But it only happens after he hears the voice of God say, "Be strong and courageous…for the LORD your God will be with you" (Joshua 1:9).

That was the lesson for me.

I wasn't Bishop X or Superintendent Y. I was James, still trying to figure out what it meant to lead in humility, with my limp visible, trusting God to fill in the gaps.

One of the hardest days of my superintendency came when I had to handle a deeply personal pastoral crisis that one of the best pastors I supervised stumbled over.

A colleague, someone I loved, was caught in an embarrassing situation that resulted in difficult consequences. It was public. Painful. Messy. And suddenly, I was no longer James, their friend. I was James, the authority.

I remember praying in the car on the way to their home, asking God for strength and grace. And I remember sitting in the study, looking them in the eye, and saying, "I love you, but we have to walk through this."

We both wept.

That conversation changed me. Because that day, I had a choice. I could handle it like a bureaucrat or a brother. I could be a supervisor, or I could do my job but still be a shepherd. And for the first time in a long time, I felt like a pastor again. One of the best days of my work as a superintendent was seeing this pastor fully restored and placed back into full-time ministry as a healed, strong, and gifted pastoral leader.

I also learned that spiritual leadership isn't about being right. It's about being surrendered.

In his letters to the Corinthians, Paul often spoke about leadership through weakness: "Therefore I will boast all the more gladly about my weaknesses, so that Christ's power may rest on me" (2 Corinthians 12:9b). That was becoming real for me. The more honest I was with pastors, the more they responded. The more I admitted my own struggles, the more permission it gave them to be human.

It's ironic. We spend years building a résumé of spiritual strength, only to find that people are most drawn to our confession of spiritual need.

One of the things that kept me sane during those years was visiting a monastery once a year. Just me and silence.

The Trappist monks there don't speak during meals. They pray in unison, they work quietly, and they carry a peace that doesn't need performance. The first few days were always agonizing, no phone, no agenda, just solitude. But eventually, my soul would slow down. And in that stillness, God always spoke.

I remember one particular visit, walking the grounds with tears in my eyes, whispering, "God, am I really who You say I am? Because I don't feel like it."

And in that silence, a gentle reassurance: "Yes, you are. You're mine."

There was one phrase I found myself repeating in those days of spiritual re-centering: clean hands and a pure heart. Psalm 24:3–4 asks, "Who may ascend the mountain of the Lord? Who may stand in his holy place? The one who has clean hands and a pure heart." I'm embarrassed to admit it was in my first year of seminary when I discovered that text. I didn't discover it in my Bible reading. I was reading a book by Maxie Dunnam where he tells a story about his mother that has ministered to me often over the course of thirty years. While visiting his elderly parents in Perry County, Mississippi, Maxie remembers how conversations with his mother, Cora, whom the family affectionately called "Co-Bell," always returned to the Bible. Although she didn't read much toward the end of her life (she joked that her eyes were poor), she loved the Psalms, especially the thought in Psalm 24 about who may "ascend the mountain of the Lord" and the image of "clean hands and a pure heart" (Psalm 24:3–4). When Maxie would ask her to read it from an old family Bible on her coffee table, she always stopped and looked up at her son and said, "I've got clean hands." Dunnam uses his mother's quiet, faithful life as an illustration of what it means to be fit to stand in God's presence: not attention-grabbing piety but a steady, simple devotion that embodies the "clean hands and pure heart" image.

I must have thought about that story a million times over the years and have used it in many sermons. For many years, I was never brave enough to say the words, "I've got clean hands" for fear I'd be fooling myself. After all, I know who I am in the dark. I know there have been many times in my Christian walk and ministry that I didn't have clean hands or a pure heart. I'd fall back into the patterns of Western Christianity where counting "nickels and noses" far outweighed my concern for the hearts of the people in the pew. I knew my failures as a friend, husband, and father. I desperately desired to live with clean hands and a pure heart, but I condemned myself far too often. But Co-Bell Dunnam, though being in Glory many years

53

now has taught me something from her dear son's beautiful memory. It's Jesus, not my successes or even my ability to keep all ten commandments, who gives me clean hands. His love, acceptance, and sacrifice make me fit to stand before a holy God. Everything from my physical hands and brain are as "filthy rags." I have preached that so, so well. But it took a little tenant farmer's wife from Perry County, Mississippi to finally bring God's truth home to my heart.

It's not about making no mistakes. It's about living honestly without pretense.

As superintendent, I had to learn to lead not just with policies and principles but with presence and prayer. I had to unlearn control. I had to let pastors fail without trying to rescue them. I had to stop seeing myself as the answer and instead point people back to the only One who really is.

Eventually, my time as superintendent came to a close. In the Methodist system, it's a six-year appointment. And as the end drew near, I knew I was heading back to the local church.

But I was different.

I had a deeper understanding of grace. I was slower to speak and quicker to pray. I knew the names of churches that no one talked about at conference sessions but where the Spirit was alive and well. I had seen God work in storefronts, steeples, and Sunday school rooms. I'd learned the sacredness of small things.

And I carried all of it into my next assignment.

When I transitioned from the district superintendency into my next appointment, I was walking into the most difficult and demanding season of my ministry. On paper, it looked like a huge step up. A large church with a history of bold missions and ministry. A large staff. A visible platform.

But under the surface, I was stepping into a storm.

The church I was appointed to had been in decline. It had once been a beacon, but the light had dimmed. Morale was low. The staff was fractured. It was an affluent congregation so financially, things were steady but not strong, the large building in disrepair. There was a lot of work to be done.

And the weight of expectation was heavy.

It's rare for a district superintendent to be sent to a church in the same district they've overseen. But that's exactly what happened to me. I already knew the congregation. I already knew the issues.

The bishop believed I had the gifts to lead a turnaround, and I wanted to believe that, too. After all, not only had I been in the trenches of denominational foxholes, but I was a "skilled" pastor. This would be a cinch.

Some advisors recommended that I ask the entire staff to resign and reapply, essentially allowing a clean slate to rebuild the culture. But something about that didn't sit right with me. It felt cold. Corporate. Not pastoral. After weeks of prayer, I decided against it. I chose to work with the staff I inherited.

That decision would come back to haunt me.

At first, it felt like an opportunity of a lifetime. I was finally stepping fully into the role of mentor, not just mentee. I had watched young pastors I'd mentored flourish in ministry, and it gave me great joy. But I thought maybe this season would be marked by multiplication, not just in church size or budget but in people. In hearts. In leaders.

I wanted to be a Nathan. A Jonathan. I wanted to kneel beside colleagues and say, "I'm not here to control you, I'm here to serve you." I actually did that physically a few times. Because the world of Christianity is often a rote exercise, it frightened people. We talk a good game, but we respect alpha leaders, not shepherds with dirty hands and feet.

Serving was my priority. I meant it, and I preached it. But something unexpected happened. As I tried to let go of the mask and be real, be James not Reverend Williams, it didn't always draw people closer. It scared them. In some ways, it pushed them away.

I've always said the most successful, gifted businesspeople often lose their minds in the world of the church. Everything is tied to spirituality and to God. The devil uses the emotional immaturity of many staff and lay leaders of churches—especially those with great influence and potential. It's often subtle and quiet. It's not about bad people, but the enemy is slick. And his greatest weapon is the human ego.

I had always longed to be more open, more emotionally honest. I wanted staff meetings that weren't just about calendars and budgets but were also about calling and soul care. I wanted real conversations about what it meant to follow Jesus, not just as employees of a church but as humans with a deep yearning for the things of God. Our congregations deserve that. Not perfect staff but deeply committed staff. I truly believed that I could have hard, sometimes troubling, confidential conversations with staff in order to hit spiritual growth and healing head on. I had grown so weary of careful, political dynamics that assured us the largest donors would remain so. I stopped caring about keeping people just so my financial and attendance statistics rose. I wanted to build a team that could see the difficult problems and personalities of the church with the eyes of Christ. But I have to be honest, I found very few staff who could handle that level of honest work. It's much easier to just "smile pretty and say 'Jesus'" and to ignore the muck and mire that inevitably makes its way into the local church. Facing toxicity and dealing with healthy conflict, I found, was almost impossible in a place where it should be modeled for an unchanged, spiritually dying world. I exhausted myself trying to be real. I'm still at times unsure what that even means. I truly wanted real, even when it might hurt. I wasn't afraid of temporary pain in order to see a healthy body come to fruition. My deepest desire was to love even when it was very uncomfortable.

But not everyone wants that. And not everyone knows what to do with that. The corporate model has been welcomed in the world of the church more than the Acts model, where death, destruction, undying commitment, and emotional turmoil eventually, under the power of the Holy Spirit, give way to the path to the Cross. I was in a large church with a growing congregation and a staff to lead. I knew the expectations. I understood the culture. I had learned how to speak the "language" of pastoral leadership, vision, alignment, systems, and discipleship pathways. And I believed in all of it.

But I also knew I was in danger of trading authenticity for admiration.

There's a strange tension that pastors live in; we're called to lead, to be strong and clear, but also to be broken and real. When that tension is ignored, when we lean too far into competence and too far away from vulnerability, we become spiritual caricatures.

I had learned to walk with the Spirit. I journaled. I prayed. I had mentors. But I was still trying to be the image of the professional pastor that American church culture loves. Polished. Passionate. Unshakably confident.

I began to realize that some people don't want a shepherd; they want a spiritual CEO. They want a pastor who is shiny, efficient, and predictable with interesting sermons. One that does not in any way reveal his or her over- and side-steps. The Bible is full of people who made horrendous decisions, yet God redeemed and restored them at their moment of repentance. I've never committed any of the "deal breaker" pastor sins, but I had given in to the Western model of pastoring. To me, that's worse. Blatant sin can be worked through and turned around. Pride and influence are rewarded—but sins nonetheless if it undermines true calling. As I share boldly and transparently with you in these pages, I must admit I still live with heartache around the fact that some of what I am describing is just the way it will always be. Our church culture runs so deep it will be too difficult for some congregations and pastors to change. I currently pastor, and it's still hard work. Every day, without fail, I ask myself how I can love in spite of having to have difficult conversations. I have become much more aware of having to die daily in order to remain a servant leader. It is a hard truth that many churches could never have any of the disciples or giants of the Old Testament in their church leadership. Those congregations, in the twenty-first century, will remain impotent while churches that err on the side of grace will see life transformation and true baptisms, not just "water-dips" to gain privileged church membership.

Though my heart has always been right, I had the polished pastor thing down pat. I used it to navigate the power plays, legalists, and gossipmongers in order to keep the peace while I tried to do ministry on the side. I can't believe I just admitted that, but if you're a pastor, you get it. No more. I was done acting the part. I needed real, and so did they. It was terrifying. A pastor I greatly respect knew my heart in this. I remember him one day saying, "Be careful. People will study you. Don't give them too much of yourself. It could backfire." It did. But I'd do it again just in a more transparent, deeper way. At night, I'd lie in bed and think about how Jesus stayed real and in the now, even as whips laced with chips of animal bone tore across his back. I thought about the disciples, misunderstood, envied, and tortured, and how they remained fully in their calling to the end. I read all I could of saints like Martin Luther, Dietrich Bonhoffer, and Joan of Arc. All who sacrificed everything to be who they were and to lead people to do the same. No, I didn't face anything as dramatic as they did…but then again, maybe I did.

There are things worse than death to the human psyche. We live in our need for acceptance, accolades, and applause. We all enjoy it. It's natural. And especially for personalities who are drawn to ministry. The concept of imago Dei, or "image of God," posits that every human being reflects a divine essence through capacities for reason, morality, and relationality, regardless of their societal standing. This inherent dignity forms the foundation of human worth, existing entirely independent of external validation. However, as human beings, we all enjoy external affirmation, and this desire is natural to our social nature. The profound tension of the imago Dei lies in reconciling our inherent, God-given value with our natural human longing for external recognition. Understanding this balance means recognizing that while we appreciate applause, our core identity and worth are permanently secure in our creation in God's image, not in the fluctuating opinions of others.

What makes this difficult is that we learn early on (and it often begins in seminary classrooms) to use honey and not vinegar in order to gain more souls for the Kingdom. And it's easy to justify. Too easy. I drank that Kool-Aid; not only did I drink it, I bought extra to freeze and make popsicles! I was all in. The human condition, though always redeemable, still longs for approval. But God is a jealous God. Talk about transparent, God told us that Himself. God knows our need for approval and praise. So does the enemy. It can be and is so often a double-edged sword. But what I found was that being real was the only way I felt close to God. Though it was hard and not often appreciated, I could be true to my call and the message of the cross and actually make a long-term difference in people's lives instead of the flash and dash of the American model of "church."

I was learning that when I stopped performing, I lost the applause. But I gained something better.

I gained peace.

Not right away. But eventually.

I remember driving home late one night after a long and somewhat unproductive council meeting. I had been pastoring these people for almost seven years and through some of the biggest obstacles in my personal life and the world. I had just been contacted about the possibility of taking a new position in another large church a few states away. I was tempted, especially after a meeting like that one, but I no longer wanted to cut bait and run. I was determined to grow and struggle alongside the people God had given me. The problem was making good people with bad habits understand why we needed to lead with the heart of Christ and not the Fortune 500! Sitting in the car in our driveway, staring out the windshield with the lights off, I said out loud, "God, I don't know if I can keep doing this. But I know You called me."

It wasn't dramatic. No booming voice answered. No sudden revelation. But peace washed over me. A stillness that didn't erase the pain but reminded me I wasn't alone.

That's been the story of my life, really.

God doesn't always give me answers.

But He gives me Himself.

And that's enough.

REFLECTION FOR THE PASTOR'S HEART:

How has your past influenced how you pastor?

What fires have you walked through along the way?

In what ways have you felt misplaced in your ministry or confirmed that you were in the right place?

Do you seek the accolades of performance or the peace of presence?

UNRAVELING

*God will never disappoint us… If deep in our hearts we suspect
that He will, we are not yet convinced that He is love.*

–St. Augustine

I learned many years ago that one can feel deeply, I mean 100 percent, that God is able, willing, and has every difficulty under control and is steering toward a good, gracious, and abundant outcome, yet live and act totally opposite to that in worry, anxiety, and behavior. We humans are a complex bunch. The Augustine quote above is true but not always. I've lived in faith and doubt at the same time. Haven't you? In ministry, it's even more complex because there is a very real expectation from those to whom we minister for us to be role models of great faith. There is a song by the group Lifehouse titled simply, "Flight." It's a beautiful ballad about a spiritual struggle and the confusion we can sometimes live in as people who are called to "be" Jesus as a vocation. I can relate to the following words:

> *Your eyes are like lightning*
> *Your voice is like water*
> *This place is a desert*
>
> *I've been walking in circles*
> *I'm screaming for answers*
> *I might fall into pieces*
> *Or maybe I'm finally breaking through*

And I need you now
There's too many miles on my bones
I can't carry the weight of the world
No, not on my own.[1]

It's true, isn't it? We can know God fully and still live in the dry places of heaviness and confusion. The night of the council meeting was not when that struggle started in me. I began to yearn and dig for ways to help the church be the true church when I was coming to the end of my days as a district superintendent.

Not only was I on my way to lead a difficult turnaround in what had been one of the strongest congregations in Methodism, but as the early signs of the crumbling of the United Methodist Church as I knew it began, I found myself standing there, front and center and in the middle of what was to become a war that I never could have predicted.

Though I left the bishop's cabinet, I was asked to remain on his executive team, which was charged with creating a plan for our state as we faced the inevitable splintering that ensued. My tenure in denominational administration had taught me more than I ever expected: how to lead, how to mediate, and how to stand in the tension between pastors, congregations, and the institution itself. I came out of those six years sharper, more experienced, and more resolute. I had grown as a leader.

But emotionally? I was depleted. And spiritually, I felt strong as ever, but I was about to be tested in a way I had never known.

As I said earlier, I stepped into what would become my most difficult ministry assignment yet: a prominent congregation with a large staff, a long, impressive history, and eyes on every move we made. As I mentioned earlier, I had served this congregation already as their superintendent, an unusual scenario. I knew many of the is-

---

1. Lyrics from "Flight" by Lifehouse, *Out of the Wasteland*, 2014.

sues. I knew the undercurrents. But nothing could have prepared me for the reality of what came next.

When the bishop asked me to step into the role as lead pastor, I prayed. And I hesitated. I'd always dreamed of planting a church, starting from scratch and building something shaped around the Acts community. But that wasn't what was offered. And I said yes to my new assignment.

If you're a pastor reading this, you understand the paradoxes. I learned to navigate those paradoxes, even to ignore them, sometimes at my peril. But I was proud that I could juggle all of the balls. After I left the district superintendency, spinning plates became my life. I often joke that not only is leading through chaos not my first rodeo, but also, I often felt like the clown!

As I walked back into the local church after years in a direction-less denomination, trying to do my part to bring clarity to our future and the true meaning of scriptural authority, I was surrounded by good and gracious people. But I had just as many unwise personalities constantly at my heels. I never expected perfection or even an extremely healthy environment. I just wanted to serve and preach the Gospel with my whole heart.

What I really became was a CEO and excellent marketeer. I became a public relations agent for the United Methodist Church. It was unfair to me *and* the congregation. In my first three years in my new church, I spent over 600 hours working on denominational committees getting us ready for disaffiliation. I felt like the Wizard in the *Wizard of Oz*. I was living the decimation of the denomination behind the scenes but would stand in the pulpit each week basically saying, "Pay no attention to the man behind the curtain." Or do you remember as a child going to have your portrait taken, and the photographer would shake a stuffed animal over his head, so you'd be distracted from the actual photo. I was the photographer, and I was too good at it, and it took its toll.

At first, I felt hope, like this might be the moment I had waited for my whole ministry. I'd moved from being mentored to mentoring. I saw younger pastors stepping into their call, and I wanted to be for them what others had been for me: a servant not a spotlight seeker. Someone who believed in them, encouraged them, and walked with them through the fire.

I wanted real friendships. Paul and Timothy. Jesus and John and Peter. I didn't want the masks anymore. I yearned for relationships where we could support one another to the hilt, butt heads but love deeply, and forgive one another's weaknesses in order to grow stronger in Christ. *That* was real ministry to me. But I was a part of a system that soothed the unhealthy behaviors of some and moved people on to the next place instead of staying in the foxholes as brothers and sisters in Christ. It was confusing and felt like a life of insincerity that was dedicated to manufactured harmony above all else.

And in my personal life, I was growing. My marriage was strong. My children were finding their way in the world. I was learning how to be a more present father and a more attentive husband.

But in ministry, as I pulled back the curtain, it seemed to expose people's fears. As I stopped performing and started being more human, more vulnerable, the opposite of what I expected began to unfold. I stopped focusing on saving face and keeping the conflict at bay. I revealed my own struggles and vulnerabilities for the first time in a deep way. It was terrifying, yet God was giving me freedom I had not experienced in all my years in ministry.

Instead of trust, there was suspicion.

Instead of connection, there was silence.

Instead of friendship, there was control.

I gave all my trust upfront instead of allowing people to earn it as I had done in the past. I promoted inexperienced people in order to celebrate their successes and growth with them. That was Jesus, I thought. I was doing something not perfect but mostly right.

Though there were ugly events and stresses, I believed God would fill in the gaps for us. We were learning together to be an Acts 29 community.

And then the storm hit.

What I didn't know at the time was that I didn't yet know how to serve the people closest to me. Not really. I wanted to. And in many ways, I had grown. I was learning. But in trying to live more openly and vulnerably, it was as if I scared people away instead of drawing them close.

I wasn't fully aware that my presence carried more weight sometimes than I intended. And while I tried to lead with grace, the wounds of the people around me often met the wounds inside of me. That's dangerous chemistry.

The church I stepped into had been through hardship. Financial struggle. Internal tension. But thanks to the very difficult work of my predecessors, the foundation was still stable enough to be open to a new way. A huge debt had just been retired but there was little money in reserves when I arrived. Over several years, our budget increased greatly as a result of generous giving. We grew. We obtained and launched a second campus. We baptized people. Lives were transformed.

But underneath the surface, there was instability that statistics couldn't fix.

Our denomination was unraveling, not in theory but in real-time. There were theological debates that had simmered for decades. After the pandemic, they exploded. Pastors were turning on each other. Laypeople were divided. Bishops were at odds. Congregations were disaffiliating. Racism and "justice" and "social-focused" theology came to very public blows, even in churches. It was ugly. The very fabric of our connectional system was being shredded.

And I was pastoring one of the most high-profile churches in the Southeast.

The media called. I knew how to handle that, my early background in communications had trained me well. But what I wasn't prepared for was the emotional strain of trying to shepherd a somewhat theologically diverse congregation through something they never imagined they'd have to face.

Some were desperate to remain United Methodist. Others were ready to leave. And both sides were deeply convicted. This wasn't apathy. It was anguish.

I prayed. Hard. I preached. Harder. I tried to be a voice of unity. But I also had convictions. I wasn't trying to burn bridges, but I did start walking around with a fire extinguisher in my back pocket. I was trying to walk in truth. My strategic management and closed-door meetings with staff were seen as secretive, and when I was just trying to hold down the fort and respect all of the views coming at me daily, it was seen as not being transparent. It wasn't true, but I received a hard lesson that perception is reality, and when bad theology meets envy, there are wars of biblical proportions.

Eventually, we held a vote. A large majority decided to disaffiliate. The largest majority of any other disaffiliating congregation in the United States at that time. The spotlight got even bigger.

That decision changed everything.

There was a shift in our leadership culture after that. Some of it I anticipated; some of it blindsided me.

The United Methodist Church, this denomination that had raised me, ordained me, and shaped me was coming apart at the seams. For decades, tension had brewed. Theological shifts, cultural divides, legislative battles. Every General Conference pushed the cracks wider until they became unbridgeable.

My leadership was being watched closely and was both praised and questioned. It felt terribly schizophrenic. And I was trying to get back to doing Kingdom work and what I was called to do. It was almost impossible. The phone rang off the hook from pastors around the country asking me how I did what I did. What would we do? How would we vote? Would we stay or would we totally disaffiliate, or join the new, fledgling denomination being born out of pain and power plays? I was demonized publicly, behind the scenes, and on social media. I'll never forget deciding to delete my Facebook account. I was so tired of the constant badgering and criticism. I could handle it. It's part of leadership. But I didn't have to give it my own forum! My teenage daughter said, "Dad, you can't delete Facebook; you have over 5,000 friends!"

I asked, "Do I really?" I'm not sure I would've described all of those followers as friends.

The tension in the pews became a weight I carried daily. I had members begging me to stay. Others warned we must leave. Many didn't understand why it mattered so much.

It was lonely. It was heavy. One day, I'd get a letter or email affirming my leadership. I walked on water. The next day, someone would question my leadership and decisions and question whether I was a tool of Satan—or even Satan himself. It was a time like no other. And I was leading in the dark.

Still, I kept preaching. I kept praying. I kept trying to hold it all together.

But a short while after the vote, something shifted, subtly at first but undeniably.

The staff dynamic changed. Loyalties disappeared. The culture started to unravel. We continued, even through the difficulties, to grow in number and financially. *We can get through this*, I thought. I counted it all as growing pains, but I was surrounded by people who were awash in uncertainty, suspicion, and duplicity.

One of the staff pastors I had inherited was leading discipleship ministries, but I immediately saw him as the main associate pastor I needed early in my ministry there, someone I trusted deeply. He was compassionate, smart, and grounded. He was only in his forties but a strong husband and father. His family came first, something I had not learned to do until much later in ministry. He told me the truth when others would not. When there were gaps in my drive or leadership, he called them out, not with shame but in brotherhood. We didn't talk about it much, but we both knew his time as an associate wouldn't last. He had strong gifts and loved Jesus and people with a passion. Like me, he was second career and had a background in management with an MBA. I knew he was being shaped to lead his own congregation. He was born to lead a church, and soon, he did.

When he left to take on a senior pastorate in the new denomination in another state, I wasn't surprised, and he went with my blessing. But I lost more than a staff member. I lost a friend by my side. A partner.

And the unraveling deepened.

I began to experience some things I had never experienced. I had never felt such severe loneliness and constant uncertainty in my work. It had become all too obvious to me and to some in lay leadership that I had trusted some staff too deeply without regard for previous experience and left some in places where they absolutely could not grow a ministry or themselves. That was my mistake and, in many ways, naivete. For the first time, I'd decided to throw all caution to the wind and reward eagerness instead of results. I still believe that's right to a point. I spent almost a year studying the leadership of Jesus. He trusted the most unlikely of people. As he called the disciples to follow, they had all kinds of "red flags" that he looked past. It's definitely a Jesus model, but the American view of hiring and investment is the total opposite. I felt caught between my business acumen and New Testament risk and grace.

Ministry is not done with a business formula. It's much more art than skill. I had decided I'd trust the Holy Spirit with the gaps. I had fallen into a trap I thought I never would. One of my seminary professors told a story about their early years in ministry working with a young ministerial student. When asked why they had not turned in their sermon manuscript before preaching the sermon assignment to their classmates, the student responded, "I don't write sermons. I walk into the pulpit and allow the Holy Spirit to speak through me!" To which my professor replied, "It's a shame you don't give the Holy Spirit more to work with." I remember thinking that would never be me. And it wasn't as far as preaching. But I had blamed the Holy Spirit for not laying better groundwork with some staff. I learned a valuable lesson. There's no substitute for preparation and experience. My heart was right, but my guidance was needed along with my trust. The environment had changed in all of our stress and strain of navigating the denominational unrest. I had begun to take shortcuts I said I'd never take. The people I had loved, served, and prayed with were slipping away. Some had changed. Some said I had changed. Everyone had their story.

And I was questioning everything I thought I had decided on firmly.

I prayed and called out to God often in those days. I sat in my office late at night, praying, journaling, and wondering what had happened. I tried everything I knew. I tried silence. I tried clarity. I tried strategy.

But nothing worked.

I was more excited about ministry than I'd ever been but dealt daily with a gnawing inner conflict about where and how I was serving. The people I had once fought for and led so well, I now found myself trying to survive alongside.

And that's when it came: the realization that it was time to go. The church leadership would be forced into a decision by me. I only blamed myself.

I didn't want a celebration. I didn't want a farewell sermon. I just wanted to slip away quietly. I wanted to pray. I wanted to sit beside Natalie and ask God what in the world He was doing. For the first time in my life, I made a decision to leave a congregation instead of fighting to stay. My ministry had been made up of long and, quite frankly, successful tenures. I had never asked a bishop to move me. In the past, I had never been ready to move. I had no experience in this. I had no bishop to blame. It was grueling, and I didn't know what was next.

Looking back, I needed a group of leaders who could see I needed help, rest, and grace. In that environment, in the midst of so much confusion of leaving a large denomination, I only received raised eyebrows and somewhat punitive solutions. I understood it. Their reputation was on the line. The Western church has this erroneous idea that a squeaky-clean image will help them in their plan for Kingdom work. It's a lie and, frankly, the enemy's playground. Churches that will walk with their pastors (and their families) through the fire in the twenty-first century will make the greatest impact for eternity. It's a simple truth that is so hard for pious, longtime church folks to grasp.

I was scheduled to go to New Delhi, India in the middle of all this chaos for a mission trip. I kept telling Natalie that I had no business leaving the country, and I needed to stay and keep navigating the ship. But I had promised to go in support of a mission there that I loved and was close to my heart. I left Kentucky on a plane that seemed to be surrounded in black and white.

When I stepped off the runway in India, the colors came back like a giant prism. It smelled like a combination of body odor, turmeric, cumin, and thick, automotive exhaust. I remembered riding the old, yellow school bus each day in the humid weather of South Carolina while we kept all of the windows down. When the bus driver hit the gas, the distinct smell of old engine smoke would fill that old bus. The air in India was even worse than that. The smog was almost unbearable. Sickness, poverty, and chaos surrounded me. Sewage ran down the streets, yet I felt like I was in the presence of a holy God like never before. The bright colors of the handmade scarves and women's sarees were like beautiful invitations to connect to something real and pure. There was no fear or confusion in me. God met me as I walked through the streets of this faraway land.

For two weeks, my team walked with some of the most loving, hospitable Christians I'd ever encountered. These were people who had to watch their every move for fear of government persecution, yet they were following Jesus boldly and without apology. The smiles of children who lived in the worst slums in Asia were like a light to my soul. I walked into one-room cubicles that were no bigger than a kitchenette in America. In the worst poverty of my country, I had never seen anything like this. For many years, I lived in government housing projects as a child. Low-income housing in the West would have almost been a mansion to the people in these slums. During our visits, my team would cram into a small area where a family of five to six people lived. The school packed children into small classrooms that were filled with the smells of burning bodies in a crematorium directly across from the school. They had so little, yet they were kind, spirit-filled, and wanted to give me everything they had.

One of my team members, Robert, and I visited with a family one afternoon, and we had both been instructed not to eat or drink anything that was offered to us because our systems may not be able to fight a foreign microbe. As we sat and conversed with this dear family through our interpreter, suddenly the mother looked at her son, who was about ten years old, and said something I couldn't understand. He ran out of the little cubby and was back within minutes carrying an opened bottle of Coca-Cola. This sweet mother poured the Coke into glasses she took from her one shelf in the whole house and handed a filled cup to me and Robert. We both looked at each other knowingly and, for a quick second, decided we'd pretend to drink from the cup. Neither of us could do that though.

I watched Robert drink that little bit of America down, and so I reluctantly did the same. That Coke would have cost this mother two days' wages. There was no way I was going to refuse her hospitality. I walked out of that place a new creature in some ways. God was convicting my pastor's heart shaped by Western excess and religious politics. I couldn't stop thinking about what I was actually doing as I prepared to go back to the states.

As I walked down the very narrow walkway, laughing children gazed at me like I was a celebrity. They were happy, almost oblivious to their poverty-stricken state that glared at me like an oversized floodlight. I smiled and waved, barely able to hold in my emotions. As I made my way back to our van, dodging people, cows, dogs, and beggars, tears ran down my face. I was too embarrassed to let the rest of the team see me crying, but I knew I was not returning to America the same man. The people's countenance was what I imagined the people in the early church must have shown. All they had was Jesus, no backup plan, no reserve funds, no bishop or cabinet to guarantee an income, no hefty pension, and certainly no freedom of religion. Yet they were sold out. They had each other, the love of family and a willingness to follow Jesus with no net. I was faced with what I had become, and I was doing it so well. But I felt like a hireling.

Over the years of living in Kentucky, I had come to deeply appreciate people who call the mountains of Eastern Kentucky home. It is, in my opinion, the most beautiful part of the commonwealth. In spite of that, there is abject poverty, a result of their most plentiful resource, coal, being mined almost totally away, along with thousands of jobs that had sustained families for hundreds of years. A pastor friend of mine who grew up and served many churches in the area once told me that many preachers were not paid by their churches. They were bi-vocational and often given gifts of food and other necessities by their congregations. They didn't believe in pastors making a salary for serving the Lord, and paid pastors were often referred to as "hirelings." I remember my haughty attitude toward that primitive viewpoint, but I must say, it was on my mind a lot while in India. As I considered the clergy pay in New Delhi, I compared my compensation with those there who had given their very lives, sometimes literally, for the Gospel.

My heart twisted inside of my chest. I returned from India knowing I was going to move on. I didn't know how or when, but a pastor just knows. The budget was strong. We were doing consistent, important ministry in the city and around the world. Sundays were beautiful, and the worship was on point. We'd just begun a major sanctuary renovation. There were people in the pews, and we were recovering well from the dark days of the pandemic. I believed I could see our two-campus ministry turn into three campuses within five years. I was becoming more impatient with typical personalities and entitled leaders who had long, much too long, tenures. It wasn't really fair to those individuals. I was the lead pastor. It was up to me to remedy those issues, but I was choosing my battles strategically and carefully so as not to offend my leadership. It was almost cowardly. In order to see "my vision" come to fruition, I was allowing people with the wrong gifts to remain in lay and staff positions when I should have faced it head on. I was both growing and struggling at the same time. I had never experienced that before. But I knew my growth was about to lead me to something different. My model was falling apart. The polished, "megachurch tricks" were making me sick. I loved this congregation too much to keep the curtain closed any longer. I was at odds with some staff and leaders. In some ways, it was an easy fix. Misunderstandings took the spotlight and I, for the first time in my whole ministry, stopped fighting. I stopped defending my decisions. I'll never forget listening to folks in leadership around me. Have you ever heard the teacher's voice in the Peanuts cartoons? That was my life for about the last three months as a leader in a place God was removing me from. God and I debated. I kept telling Him how to set my future. He didn't listen. I'm grateful He didn't.

With Natalie's blessing, I gave up everything (I thought) and went silent. That's not the norm for me. The accolades still kept coming. But my time was up. Not everyone appreciated my heart or style. That's ministry.

I knew this chapter was over.

I was deeply wounded, and I knew others were, too. People who had been like family turned against me. There are always two sides to the story, and I carry my part of the pain. But the hardest part wasn't the conflict.

The hardest part was knowing I was about to leave people I still loved.

I gave everything I had to that church. My heart. My time. My vision. And it still fell apart.

After I had returned to my office late one night to finish a sermon, I sat completely alone in a building that was over 100,000 square feet. I had been the pastor there for years, and there were still places I'd never been in the building. That night, I walked into every room, every restroom, every square inch of the basement's furnace rooms. I sat in the age-level areas and the music suite and prayed. I thanked God for allowing me to serve and for trusting me with this beautiful, diverse congregation of prayer warriors, world-renowned biblical scholars, and well-respected professionals in the community. I thought about all the baptisms, weddings, and funerals I had officiated and could describe in detail how every single one had shaped me. I had placed my hands on the heads of numerous teenagers after they completed confirmation. Just two weeks before my resignation, I preached the funeral for one of our high schoolers who had tragically drowned at a graduation party.

I knelt that night at the same altar where hundreds of teenagers had just knelt for prayer during that funeral, and I wept. My grieving started long before I had accepted my walking papers. I had never been more confused or more at peace in my entire ministry.

I walked back to my desk and reached down to the bottom of my black Samsonite bag. I had been carrying it ever since my brother-in-law, Charles, one of my dearest friends, had given it to me when I graduated from seminary. I took out a little, black moleskin notebook my friend and associate pastor, Derek, had given me before he left to serve the congregation in North Carolina. It was my journal that I had written in each night while in India, and I began to read it for the first time since I had returned home. I had written a quote in the front cover from Billy Graham that I had used in sermons many times before:

"It's God's job to judge, the Holy Spirit's job to convict, and my job to love."

It hit me like a punch in the chest. I had been trying to fix things, fix people, and carry burdens that were never mine to carry. I had loved, even loved unconditionally, but I had also tried to control.

And now it was time to lay it all down. My opportunity in my current assignment to be fully present had passed. But I knew the future could be different. That night, I gave everything back to God that I had taken from Him. I had a choice. I could fight to stay in my current pastorate and correct every error, or I could let go of the reins, place myself in the hands of the people God had given me, and trust Him for the future. For one of the first times in my ministry, I chose the latter. God gave me my answer. He was my source and my defender. In turn, I vowed to be even more present with people and my family, whether my next assignment was to another congregation or to be a greeter at Walmart. I was tired of conspicuously hiding from God and doing it my way. When my children were young, I'd often shout out, "Where's Mary Grace? Where is John?" They would cover their face with their hands and believe Daddy couldn't see them. I loved it and played it to the hilt. I'd walk around the house, shouting their names, while they walked closely behind me, face-covered like they were invisible. I had been playing that game with God. I stood up from that altar, took my hands away from my face, and vowed to walk back into my calling to be, yes *be*, with people again.

Three months before I left, I was sitting in my office with a dear friend, Matthew Sleeth. He had been chosen by *Newsweek Magazine* as one of the most influential Christians in America. But to me, he was like the brother I never had. He could see my struggle and listened intently as I expressed my confusion about the future and how I was sacrificing my family and health in order to "fix" a situation that clearly was no longer in God's plan for my future. In those turbulent years, Matthew would sit across from me with tears in his eyes, listening and supporting me in a way that was only from Jesus. He wanted nothing from me but to be there for me. I'll never forget one afternoon in my office when we talked for almost three hours. At the end, I asked him if I could pray for him. I did, and then, without missing a beat, he began praying for me. He said, "Amen," and looking up into my eyes, with tears streaming down his cheeks, he said, "James, this church will fire you for breaking nine of the commandments. But they'll give you a raise if you break one of the most important ones."

"Remember the Sabbath day by keeping it holy" (Exodus 20:8).

It hit me right between the eyes. Not only had I neglected my family, some staff, and even some church members to be a professional, distant pastor, I had also neglected God. Sabbath had become a barrier to me, precious hours in the week that I needed to accomplish my goals. It was unchristian, and it was wrong. I was a strategist. A systems thinker. I understood how large churches operated, and I was determined to lead this one well. But I was also beginning to realize that I was moving faster than my people could follow.

I had made some leadership decisions that were not healthy for my staff or me. The old adage of "hindsight is 20/20" had started to define me. I tried to give the benefit of the doubt about our current ministry model, but my blind spots had begun to affect my desire to be fully present.

I was wrong. They didn't.

And instead of adjusting, I had just tried harder. Throughout my ministry, I've worked off and on with a coach named Craig Robertson. Craig is one of the wisest people I know. He used to say that in the world of the church, we use an unhealthy formula: In order to get B, we have to do A. If A doesn't work and we don't get B, we tend to just do A harder! It's futile. But that's exactly what I had been doing. I was too proud to admit that I was leaning into futility. Just like the human body, all churches have their own DNA. Churches have their own personalities. Very few house people with evil intentions.

My experience is that all churches are filled with good people who really want to follow God's precepts. But here's the truth: If we truly follow those precepts, a lot of our lives become uncomfortable. There is sacrifice in following Jesus fully. I decided to do a bit of research. I have a dear friend who is also a brilliant physician, and I once asked him what happens to the body if it blatantly goes against its own DNA. He told me that scientifically it's very rare, but it can happen. When the human body starts to attack its own DNA, it usually means the immune system is mistakenly seeing parts of the body like cells, proteins, or even the DNA itself as threats. This mix-up can lead to autoimmune disorders and, worse, cancers. So, our immune system is built to spot dangers like viruses or bacteria by recognizing unfamiliar proteins, known as antigens. Sometimes, due to genetic factors, environmental influences, infections, or even stress, the immune system gets a bit confused and begins to target the body's own healthy tissues. If it mistakenly goes after DNA or proteins closely associated with DNA, like histones (essential proteins), it can result in inflammation, damage, and disease.

An example of this is the disease lupus. In lupus, the immune system often creates antibodies that directly attack DNA, along with other cell components. This can lead to a range of symptoms affecting the joints, skin, kidneys, brain, and more. This kind of misfire doesn't mean the DNA itself is "bad" or mutated; it just means the body is treating its own genetic blueprint like an invader. The outcome is chronic inflammation, tissue damage, and a need for ongoing treatment to manage symptoms and soothe the immune system. So, when the body turns against its own DNA, it signals that the immune system is not functioning properly, and depending on how and where this occurs, it can lead to serious chronic conditions.

Is that not a picture of the American church? We often try to fit our own human ideas into the model for what was clearly given to us in the book of Acts, and because we do that, we get nothing but dis-ease. The American church notoriously attacks its own DNA!

As a pastor, I was contributing to the disease by trying to make it comfortable to go against the true DNA.

The church began to strain. People I loved deeply began to question my leadership. I questioned it too. For the first time in decades, I wasn't sure if I could see the next season clearly. All I knew was that I couldn't go on like this.

I had one more meeting. One more night in the office.

And then I walked away. Some welcomed it; others grieved.

Leaving that congregation nearly broke me. Not because I failed but because I loved them.

Even the ones who misunderstood me.

Even the ones who were angry with me.

Even the ones I may have hurt.

I loved them.

And the moment I walked out the door for the last time felt like a death. But for the first time, I felt free.

I didn't want a farewell celebration. I didn't want a plaque. I wanted silence. I wanted solitude. I just wanted to pray and ask God, "Now what?"

Natalie and I took time to rest. Three months off with no preaching and no contact with former staff or parishioners. No emails, just rest and prayer. I realized that I had been married to the church and taken my wife for granted. I had idolized the church and ignored the Sabbath. I had chased vision and neglected presence. I thought I was invincible. I had tapped my own power and ego to keep going. I had kept driving and had been determined to be a turn-around congregation. But in that time, we remembered who we were before ministry made us feel like we had to earn God's approval.

And in the quiet of that season, God began to whisper again.

This wasn't the end. It was a new beginning.

And God in His mercy met me there.

He didn't meet me with a plan. He met me with peace. He didn't meet me with answers. He met me with love. We received hundreds of letters from people in the church and around Kentucky. People sent us gifts that overwhelmed us. Our voicemails were filled with stories of hope and redemption that God had used Natalie and me to offer.

Little did I know that those three months in which the early days felt like crucifixion would be the quiet before the resurrection. God was preparing something new. Something beautiful. Something I had dreamed of and prayed about for decades. Something I longed to lead almost every day of my ministry.

A church not built on staff or systems or status.

But on the Word. On grace.

On the Spirit.

On the real presence of Jesus.

I had finally escaped from the western tyranny of the model pastor. And what rose from those ashes was something far truer.

Far more free, I told Natalie I wanted to help build a ministry that felt like home. I left for a weeklong retreat at the Abbey of Gethsemani, a monastery I had found peace within annually for over thirty years. I laughed. I cried. I prayed. One of my dear friends in ministry, Chris Banner, showed up there to spend the day and pray with me. It was like cool water. Then, Jesus showed up and said, "James, take off your tool belt." I handed it to him in the Spirit. But I didn't want to let it go. I said, "Jesus, what will I do without it?" God took my hand and wrote these words in my journal and answered my question. The pen moved effortlessly. "Feed my sheep."

REFLECTION FOR THE PASTOR'S HEART:

In what ways have you tried to "fix" people or situations instead of simply loving and trusting God with the outcome?

Are there areas of your life where your identity is tied more to success than to surrender?

Who in your life speaks truth to you when you're tempted to chase ambition over authenticity?

What might it look like for you to take a step back and ask, "Lord, what's next?" without needing immediate answers?

"FEED MY SHEEP"

I've come a long way
I've seen how You work
There's so much goodness and grace,
Much more than I deserve
'Cause I know who I am
But I can't stay where I'm at,
We've come this far by faith,
And I just can't turn back

—*Elevation Worship*

I finally got it. I'd been trying so hard to fix sheep when all I'd been asked to do was feed them. After months of rest, prayer, and the slow work of healing, something unexpected happened.

God opened a door I had closed in my heart years ago. Over that period where I was "out of commission," I listened to a song everyday about ten times a day. It is simply titled "More Than Able." I had never heard it until a few days after my resignation. I was driving to meet my daughter for lunch, and it started playing through the car speakers. I passed the restaurant where I was to meet Mary Grace because I was weeping so much, and I knew it would worry her if I showed up like that. It became my anthem. I don't think I've gone a day since leaving Kentucky without listening to it. I'm fixated on the simple words and music. I started this chapter with the song's ending, but it starts:

When did I start to forget all of the great things You did?

When did I throw away faith for the impossible?

How did I start to believe You weren't sufficient for me?

Why do I talk myself out of seeing miracles?

You are more than able.[1]

The moment I started to believe that again, it was a reconnection with my first love, and it was then, and only then, God would say, "Now you're ready. Welcome back." I'd always longed to start something new. Not just a new program or initiative but a new congregation. A fresh expression of church built on a foundation of the Word, worship, spiritual formation, service, and deep, real community. I thought that dream had passed me by. I wasn't thirty-five anymore. I had responsibilities. I had scars. I had failures. I wasn't sure I had the energy to start from scratch.

But God does.

And He wasn't finished with me.

In the days leading up to my next assignment, I spent a lot of time with two guys that loved and accepted me as "James" and not "Rev. Williams." Mike Courtney, who pastored a large Nazarene church in Nashville, had been through his own fire and was broken down and rebuilt by the Holy Spirit. A counselor in Louisville, KY named Michael RoBards was the second person I came to heavily depend on. The day I resigned, I went straight to his office. I walked in and told him what had happened. His reply was, "Congratulations." It was unexpected, but I knew his words were from God's lips to my ears. Those two men loved me for me, looked past my weakness, and offered me Christ. They remain two of my dearest friends.

On my trip to the monastery, I received a phone call that would change my life and point me to something so outside my box it

---

1. Elevation Worship. "More Than Able." Featuring Chandler Moore & Tiffany Hudson, Elevation Worship Publishing / Maverick City Publishing, 2023.

seemed impossible. A group of deeply faithful believers in Georgia had also just been through a painful and very public splintering as a result of the denominational unrest. They had once been part of the largest United Methodist Church in the state. But like many churches around the country, they had gone through a painful season of division and loss. They had disaffiliated. Their pastor had retired. Their future was unclear.

And they wanted to talk to me.

At first, I hesitated. It felt too soon. My wounds were still healing. But Natalie and I prayed, we consulted with people we trusted and prayed some more. And the more we prayed, the more we sensed God saying, "This is it. This is the 'next.'"

We made the trip. We met with the leaders. We asked the hard questions. So did they. My interview with them was one of the most intimidating experiences of my life. They were gracious but thorough. I had spent my life going where the bishop told me to go. I had not interviewed for a job in thirty years. I had a "guaranteed appointment"—a job for life! I felt the same butterflies I'd had when I was first interviewing at advertising agencies after graduating from college thirty years earlier. I had spent years making decisions for other people, leading successful people in ministry, and calling the shots. Now, in some ways, I was starting over. I almost went into that old mode of proving I was good enough. But I stopped short. I opened myself up like I never had and trusted God 110 percent for the first time in a long time. It was beautiful.

I'd been through the pain, and I was healing. But they'd also been through a lot of pain. I sat in front of eleven of the kindest, smartest, most Christian people I had ever met. They had been hurt by an organization called to display love, joy, peace, patience, kindness, goodness, faithfulness, gentleness, and self-control. As I learned their story, I was ashamed and convicted. I knew the system. I knew how the system made decisions at times. I had made some of the same decisions that hurt this group of people as a denominational leader. It wasn't personal. It was business, at times disguised as "process," and God was always blamed for it.

How does the average person in the pew argue with that? It was the American church. That was the problem. I admitted to them my own involvement in those kinds of church problems and everything else I could remember I ever did wrong. They asked tough questions. They had me investigated and vetted more than I'd ever been in my life. They knew some things they weren't supposed to know about me. And I was glad.

There. I've only ever admitted that in these pages. I was what was wrong with the American version of church. I bought the systemic religion hook, line, and sinker, and I even benefitted from it. I was done with that. I was going to move forward authentically. I had preached it from an ivory tower. Now I had to live it. I was ready for their questions because I knew the lingo. But I didn't use it. I was open, honest, and half-hoping I wouldn't be hired. Secular businesses had my resume. Other, more established churches were wanting to talk. After hearing these leaders' pain and seeing their tears, I wanted to run! I also had my own scars. I had trauma-bonded before. I wasn't interested in doing it again. But something clicked in my spirit, and we decided to drop our guards and trust one another.

And what I found was extraordinary.

Not a church with fancy programs or a big production budget but a group of people hungry for the true God. Hungry for community. Hungry for shepherding. They didn't want polish; they wanted prayer. They didn't need flash; they needed the fire of the Holy Spirit. They didn't need perfection but presence.

PRESENCE. There it was. I had neglected being present for so long. I had important meetings to attend. I had multi-million-dollar budgets that needed to be met. I needed to pursue my vision of serving churches with multiple campuses. But in that moment, my wife's voice rang in my heart. I almost started to weep but I held back. Natalie had said to me so many times over the previous few years, "James, be in the now. Enjoy the now. Meet God in the moment." I had neglected being present. I had leaned into being what my former seminary professor, Chuck Killian, had warned me not to be: the Shell Answer Man. I needed to let down my guard and deep-seated need to fix things. This new congregation needed to let go of their hurt and open themselves to healing. That, and only that, was the "strategy" we needed.

And so, in faith, we both said yes.

That "yes" was to a new church plant: Grace Resurrection Church.

Two years before I came, a group of wandering Methodists began meeting in a small Baptist church to do nothing but support one another, study scripture, and honor God. Dr. Randy Mickler, a former football player at the University of Georgia, their former pastor, and a force in Georgia Methodism, agreed to come out of retirement and walk with them until they needed a full-time pastor. Many counted them out and predicted they would fizzle out quickly. God had another opinion! The church grew. Hurting people reluctantly showed up to see if they could really heal from the political and power wars, they had unknowingly been casualties in. Sunday after Sunday, new faces came only to love one another, their community, and lift the name of Jesus. It was glorious. They finally decided they should at least pick a name for their new community, and it was settled: Grace Resurrection. It said new life, peace, and hope. The name wasn't chosen lightly. It was born out of tears, long walks, scripture study, and the undeniable awareness that they were living into a resurrection story. Not just for the church but for every person walking through the doors looking for new life. I was hooked. I told them if they didn't hire me at minimum, Natalie and I were moving to Georgia to be a part of it. Of course, I was kidding. Sorta. My first prayer was, "God, please don't allow me to mess this up!" His Spirit was all over it.

We didn't launch with grandeur. We launched with prayer. With confession. With surrender. And in those early weeks, I saw something I hadn't seen in a long time:

Freedom. Restoration. Forgiveness. I had encountered very few church leaders who understood that.

People worshiped with open hands. People came forward for prayer without shame. People fell in love with the Word again.

And I—we—got to shepherd that.

The dream I thought I had buried had been resurrected, so to speak!

It wasn't without fear. It wasn't without resistance. Starting a church is never easy. But this was different. We weren't starting a church to compete with other churches. We were planting a church because Jesus was breathing new life into broken people, including me.

Grace Resurrection is a place for those who are done pretending.

For people who want Jesus more than titles, systems, or strategies.

For people who have been hurt by church and wonder if they can trust again.

For leaders who need to be led.

For people who've walked through fire and still believe God makes beauty from ashes.

This is not a how-to chapter.

This is a testimony.

God does not waste pain. God is not limited by systems, politics, or timelines. And when you surrender, even in brokenness, God builds something better than we could have imagined.

For me, that "better" came wrapped in a group of believers in a new place and a new opportunity to build something holy. Not perfect, but holy.

It was such a blessing that there were days I wondered if there was some catch coming. I had been praying that God would send another pastor to help me. We were growing rapidly, and I didn't want to fall back into old habits of doing so much on my own. I'd come too far to look back! I had the backing and support of four retired pastors in the congregation. All of them had served some of the largest churches in Methodism. We were a motley crew and a good team. We all had experienced the mega movements, but this was different—and God had a sense of humor. Here all five of us were in a building the size of most of the chapels from our former churches. But these guys were retired, and I needed a young pastor to help me full-time. God had removed me from one big assignment to a now monumental task.

Natalie and I began to pray about the possibility of bringing one of my associate pastors from my former church to Georgia. He and his wife were strong, courageous Christians, and they were only thirty years old. It was a pipe dream, but I gave it to God. Needless to say, God once again came through when he and his wife said, "Yes!" I had been longing to plant a new congregation with a ministry partner for many years. I'd almost given up on that dream. But I felt like the dog that chases the car every day as it passes on the road. One day, he actually caught it but didn't know what to do with it. For the first time, I was going to have to totally depend on God, humble myself, and walk it out at the Lord's pace and not my own. So, I took off the toolbelt once again, and prayed every morning, "Speak Lord, your servant is listening."

The rest of this chapter is for you, the reader. Whether you're clergy or laity, leader or learner, burned out or just beginning, I want to offer some truths that God has shown me. These are not polished principles. These are soul-tested convictions.

LIVING AS A MODEL OF JESUS, NOT JUST A MODEL OF SUCCESS

1. Surrender your identity.

In a world that tells us our worth is tied to our résumé, our reputation, or our particular set of struggles, we have to choose a different path. Christian leaders are at their strongest when their core identity is anchored in Christ alone. Ministry culture can sometimes reward charisma and production, while quietly excusing spiritual decay, and that's a dangerous trap. When leaders forget who they are in Jesus, the soul of the ministry begins to hollow out. True transformation starts when we stop performing and start surrendering.

> *Therefore, if anyone is in Christ, he is a new creation. The old has passed away; behold, the new has come.*
>
> *–2 Corinthians 5:17 ESV*

2. Your mess ups can be your step ups!

Ministry is a sacred place where people need your real and honest stories about how you were before applying God's truths fully to your life and what it looks like now that we finally say yes to His precepts. The Bible is a book full of "before and after stories." Never be ashamed of your past when God uses it to provide hope and restoration.

> *I will repay you for the years the locusts have eaten…*
>
> *–Joel 2:25*

3. You are not your title. You are not your resume. You are not the size of your congregation or the scope of your influence.

We forget this faster than we'd like to admit. Pastors often carry the pressure to validate their calling by producing visible results, and it wears down the soul. What actually defines us is the voice of the Father, who calls us His children long before He calls us His servants. I bought into the idea that ministry impact was measured by how big I could build something, and it nearly buried me. Jesus constantly proved that the unnoticed, the small, and the overlooked often carried the greatest weight in the Kingdom. Even with our modern tools and platforms, God still chooses the humble to shape the church.

If anyone would come after me, let him deny himself and take up his cross daily and follow me.

—Luke 9:23 ESV

4. Make the Word your foundation.

Every other foundation eventually shifts, disappoints, or collapses. The Word of God is the only ground firm enough to hold the weight of real ministry. When Scripture is our home base, our decisions, preaching, and leadership stop drifting with the opinions around us. You can feel the difference in your spirit when the Bible is informing your ministry instead of your ministry trying to inform the Bible. It's where clarity, conviction, and courage are born.

I will never forget your precepts, for by them you have preserved my life.

—Psalm 119:93

5. Not trends. Not podcasts. Not leadership books. The Word of God. Preach it. Live it. Submit to it.

Resources are helpful, but they're not the well we draw life from. Too many leaders have confused inspiration with revelation. Podcasts can spark ideas, but only Scripture can form a soul. When the Word becomes your authority—not just in theory, but in practice—you stop chasing every wave of novelty. That stability becomes a witness to the people you serve.

All Scripture is God-breathed and is useful for teaching, rebuking, correcting and training in righteousness, so that the servant of God may be thoroughly equipped for every good work.

—2 Timothy 3:16–17

89

6. Pursue depth over width.

We all feel the pull to reach more people, but Jesus never confused reach with impact. A ministry stretched too thin can look impressive but offer very little strength. Depth requires patience, vulnerability, and a willingness to sit with people through the slow work of spiritual formation. When you commit to depth, you start building disciples instead of spectators. What grows from that kind of investment lasts.

> *"Yet there are some of you who do not believe." For Jesus had known from the beginning which of them did not believe and who would betray him. He went on to say, "This is why I told you that no one can come to me unless the Father has enabled them." From this time many of his disciples turned back and no longer followed him.*

> *—John 6:64–66*

7. The model of Jesus was not mass production; it was deep, intentional discipleship.

He poured Himself into a few so they could reach many. That kind of ministry requires time, relationship, and the courage to walk closely with people in their mess. Invest in individuals even when it feels inefficient. Choose transformation over applause and substance over spectacle. You'll discover that real fruit grows from the slow work of abiding.

> *I am the vine; you are the branches. If you remain in me and I in you, you will bear much fruit; apart from me you can do nothing.*

> *—John 15:5*

8. Refuse to lead alone.

Isolation is one of the quickest paths to burn out and one of the enemy's favorite strategies. Leadership can be lonely, but it doesn't have to be. When you walk without support, you end up carrying burdens you were never meant to carry alone. Ministry becomes healthier the moment you choose connection over self-reliance. God designed leaders to live in community, not in shadows.

Two are better than one, because they have a good return for their labor: If either of them falls down, one can help the other up. But pity anyone who falls and has no one to help them up.

—Ecclesiastes 4:9–10

9. Build your circle of trusted friends and mentors. Invite others into your journey. Be known. Be accountable. But do this very carefully.

Do not ever cast your pearls before swine. I learned this the hard way. However, every leader needs voices who can challenge, comfort, and correct without fear. These relationships keep us grounded when success tempts us or hardship overwhelms us. Being known is uncomfortable but essential for spiritual health. Accountability is not a threat; it's a gift. Even Jesus surrounded Himself with companions.

And he appointed twelve (whom he also named apostles) so that they might be with him and he might send them out to preach.

—Mark 3:14 ESV

10. Embrace your limits.

We often behave as if healthy boundaries are signs of weakness, but they're actually signs of maturity. You are not the Savior, and pretending to be will only exhaust you and mislead others. Limits protect your heart, your family, and your calling. God isn't asking you to be everything; He's asking you to be faithful. Rest is part of obedience, not an interruption to it.

But Jesus often withdrew to lonely places and prayed.

—Luke 5:16

11. Sabbath is holy.

You are not infinite. You are not tireless. Rest is not a reward; it's obedience. Leaders forget this because we're so accustomed to running on empty. Sabbath isn't a luxury for the undisciplined—it's God's reminder that the world keeps spinning without our constant management. When we rest, we confess that God is God and we are not. There's freedom in accepting that truth. Your ministry becomes healthier when your soul is rested.

> *Remember the Sabbath day by keeping it holy. Six days you shall labor and do all your work, but the seventh day is a Sabbath to the LORD your God. On it you shall not do any work, neither you, nor your son or daughter, nor your male or female servant, nor your animals, nor any foreigner residing in your towns. For in six days the LORD made the heavens and the earth, the sea, and all that is in them, but he rested on the seventh day. Therefore the Lord blessed the Sabbath day and made it holy.*
>
> *—Exodus 20:8–11*

12. Learn to let go.

Control is one of our favorite illusions (yes, especially in ministry). We think if we just plan better or work harder, everything will fall into place. But some situations require surrender more than strategy. Letting go is often the most spiritual thing you can do. It creates room for grace, healing, and God's timing to do what our effort cannot.

> *Be still, and know that I am God; I will be exalted among the nations, I will be exalted in the earth.*
>
> *—Psalm 46:10*

13. Not everything can be fixed.

Trying to fix everything will eventually break you. Some conflicts simply require space, prayer, and the Spirit's intervention. Not every conflict can be resolved. You're responsible for faithfulness, not outcomes. Release what you cannot control. Forgive what needs for-giving. Forgiveness frees you from carrying weights that were never meant to stay on your shoulders. Peace comes when you trust God with what's beyond your reach.

> *If it is possible, as far as it depends on you, live at peace with everyone.*
>
> *—Romans 12:18*

14. Love people, not outcomes.

Ministry becomes distorted when results matter more than souls. Real success looks like people who are slowly learning to love Jesus and reflect His character. When you love people well, the numbers may or may not follow, but the Kingdom will grow. Churches built on compassion outlast churches built on metrics. Faithfulness to people always honors God more than fixation on results.

> *If I speak in the tongues of men or of angels, but do not have love, I am only a resounding gong or a clanging cymbal. If I have the gift of prophecy and can fathom all mysteries and all knowledge, and if I have a faith that can move mountains, but do not have love, I am nothing. If I give all I possess to the poor and give over my body to hardship that I may boast, but do not have love, I gain nothing.*
>
> *—1 Corinthians 13:1–3*

15. Success is not more bodies in the pews or more zeros in the budget.

We have to redefine what winning looks like. A church can be full and still spiritually empty. Winning is changed hearts, restored lives, and people who look more like Jesus. The fruit God cares about is the kind that transforms character and heals brokenness. Com-passion, justice, humility—these are the signs of a healthy church. When we chase these things, we align ourselves with God's heart.

> *He has shown you, O mortal, what is good. And what does the LORD require of you? To act justly and to love mercy and to walk humbly with your God.*

> —*Micah 6:8*

16. Don't lose your first love.

Ministry can be so consuming that we forget the One who called us to it. When love for Jesus fades, everything else becomes mechanical, pressured, and hollow. The most important work you can do is tending your own affection for Christ. Return to Him again and again until your heart softens and your joy rekindles. Nothing in leadership matters if you lose that center. Stay close to Jesus. Not ministry, not reputation, but Jesus. Preach to yourself. Repent often. Keep your eyes fixed on Him.

> *Yet I hold this against you: You have forsaken the love you had at first. Consider how far you have fallen! Repent and do the things you did at first. If you do not repent, I will come to you and remove your lampstand from its place.*

> —*Revelation 2:4–5*

We are all in process.

You may not be planting a church. You may never stand in a pulpit. But wherever God has placed you—your home, your workplace, your neighborhood—there is a calling.

God's not asking you to be famous.

He's asking you to be faithful.

And if you're willing to die to self, to let go of the pastor costume and to remove the masks, the church leader performance, and the perfection, then resurrection is possible.

Not just for churches.

But for you.

THE PROMISE OF RESTORATION

Be strong and courageous, because you will lead these people to inherit the land I swore to their ancestors to give them.

—God to Joshua (Joshua 1:6)

As I've entered my thirtieth year of ministry, I've had to come to terms with the fact that I've preached restoration while giving myself permission not to experience it. But as I've experienced a restart of sorts in my own ministry, I've been celebrating the fact that the beautiful promise of restoration is now a part of my story and the story of the church I'm privileged to pastor. This promise goes beyond the walls of our church and touches the lives of individuals and families in great ways.

In many cases, the restoration we see is not what we may expect at all. It may be in a small act of generosity, in a turn of a conversation that changes things totally, or in an instant of grace that turns a life around. I have been a witness to the large-scale results of restoration which have played out in the lives of those who enter our church.

Looking back, I must admit, community really flipped my whole life and ministry upside down (in the best way possible, honestly). All those ups and downs? The wild, messy, in-between stuff? It was always the people around me who kept me from totally losing my mind. Seriously, if I didn't have folks walking with me, calling me out, picking me up, I'd probably have burned out years ago.

In launching Grace Resurrection Church, we figured out really quickly that we weren't just putting together another Sunday country club. No way. We were building a real community of real people. One of the phrases the congregation has gotten used to hearing me say is, "There are no perfect people allowed at Grace Resurrection." It wasn't about having a slick website or perfect coffee or even flawless sermons. It was about being real, like, ugly cry real. Nobody here has it all together. We brought our baggage, our difficult stories, and our screw-ups. And that was actually the best part. I had worked to do the perfect church thing for too long. As I examined the early church and all the personalities of scripture, I was more and more awestruck by the fact that the imperfections of their lives shed light on the goodness of God and beautiful ways that healing created greater and deeper faith.

Tony Campolo has been one of my favorite preachers over the years. In his book *The Kingdom of God Is a Party*, he tells the true story of an experience he had in Honolulu, Hawaii. He was there to speak at a conference, and after landing very early in the morning, all he wanted was some rest and something to eat. A small diner was still open; it was greasy, unsanitary, and disgusting, but it was the only place he could find.

At 3:30 a.m., while Tony was sitting at the counter, eating his donut and drinking his coffee, eight or nine prostitutes entered and, since it was a small place, sat down on either side of him. They were loud, crude, and boisterous, but just as Tony was about to make his escape, the woman next to him, Agnes, told her friend that her thirty-ninth birthday was tomorrow. When her 'friend' asked nastily what she wanted her to do about it, Agnes said, "I don't want anything from you. I mean, why should you give me a birthday party?

I've never had a birthday party in my whole life. Why should I have one now?"[1]

That was when Tony made his decision. After the prostitutes had left, he called over the man behind the counter (Harry) and asked him if the prostitutes, especially Agnes, came in every night, and upon hearing that they did, he asked what Harry would say to them throwing her a birthday party, right there, tomorrow night. Harry thought it was a great idea, and they agreed that he would bake the cake and Tony would take care of the decorations.

The next day, at 2:30 in the morning, Tony returned and decorated the diner with crepe paper and a big cardboard sign that read "Happy birthday, Agnes!" By 3:15, the place was packed with prostitutes. Right at 3:30, Agnes and her friend arrived, and everyone yelled, "Happy birthday!"

Agnes was stunned. By the time they finished singing and the cake was brought out, she was openly crying. Harry had to blow the candles out for her. Then, instead of cutting the cake and eating it, Agnes asked if she could take it home and keep it. When Harry said she could, she promised she'd be right back, picked up the cake, and carrying it very carefully, walked out the door.

Everyone was silent. Nobody knew what to do. Tony broke the silence by offering to pray.

> **Looking back on it now, it seems more than strange for a sociologist to be leading a prayer meeting with a bunch of prostitutes in a diner in Honolulu at 3:30 in the morning. But then it just felt like the right thing to do. I prayed for Agnes. I prayed for her salvation. I prayed that her life would be changed and that God would be good to her.**

> **When I finished, Harry leaned over the counter and with a trace of hostility in his voice, he said, "Hey! You never told me you were a preacher. What kind of church do you**

---

1. Campolo, Tony. *The Kingdom of God Is a Party.* Thomas Nelson Publishers, 1992.

belong to?" In one of those moments when just the right words came, I answered, "I belong to a church that throws birthday parties for whores at 3:30 in the morning."

Harry waited a moment and then almost sneered as he answered, "No you don't. There's no church like that. If there was, I'd join it. I'd join a church like that!"[2]

Here's the truth: Community is the way we get the Gospel into the hearts of people. Over the years, I tried to substitute community for large events, good preaching, and six-week Bible studies. There's nothing inherently wrong with any of those things. But they are not substitutes for real relationships. I'll be honest, growing up, I didn't have much of a "community." My family bounced around a lot, which meant a whole lot of "nice to meet you" and not much "I'm here for you." Connections felt temporary. Trust? Ha! That was a foreign language. But somewhere along the way, God (in His classic, plot-twist fashion) started stitching people into my life who stuck around. Turns out, He had something better than loneliness in mind, go figure.

The early days at Grace Resurrection? They were sometimes wild and wooly. Our first Vacation Bible School only had 10 kids. I was used to over 500 kids at VBS. Sunday services, home vision meetings, prayer groups, half the time we didn't know what we were doing, but it felt like we were building something real. People actually showed up as themselves. We shared everything, the messy pain, the goofy joy, personality conflicts, all the doubts, all the hope. It felt like the family I'd always wanted but never had.

There was one Sunday that I can't forget. After this worship service that was deeply spiritual and glorious, Sarah, a new attender, comes up to me. She looks different. Not just teary-eyed but like she finally let her guard down. "Pastor James," she says, voice shaking, "I've never felt like I belonged anywhere before. But here? Here, I feel

2. Campolo, Tony. *The Kingdom of God Is a Party.* Thomas Nelson Publishers, 1992.

seen. I feel loved." I mean, come on. If that doesn't punch you right in the heart, check your pulse.

That's when it hit me. Church isn't just about showing up, singing nice songs, and hearing a polished sermon. It's about actually seeing each other, carrying each other's junk, and loving each other even when it's messy. We're in this together; there are no spectators and no sidelines.

So, here's what I've learned about community, in no particular order (and not pretending like I've got it all figured out):

- Community is like a safety net. When stuff gets rough, it catches you. The early church? They got this. Acts says they hung out, ate together, prayed, and helped each other out and nobody had to fake it. When life crashed down, they had each other.

- People make you better. No, really. You can't grow alone, not for long. "Iron sharpens iron," the proverb says, and as cheesy as that sounds on a t-shirt, it's absolute truth. Being around other people's ideas, their faith, their weird quirks, it stretches you.

- Accountability's a big deal. The world's got a weird obsession with "doing your own thing," but honestly, we need people keeping us honest. When I let others into my mess, I stay grounded. Sometimes they call me out, sometimes they hype me up, but it keeps me on track.

- Community is how the world sees Jesus. Jesus said people will know we're His by how we love each other. That's not just a nice slogan. It's the real deal. If we can't love each other, what are we even doing?

We've made it a point to actually live this out at Grace Resurrection. We've started small groups that are super relaxed, just people hanging out, eating snacks, talking Scripture, praying, and being real. We've made it mandatory to get outside the walls of a building because loving our neighbors isn't optional if you're following Jesus. And you know what? We laugh a lot. We eat a lot, too. I think Jesus would approve. There are only two rules at Grace Resurrection: 1) No perfect people are allowed and 2) You must already have or desire to have a servant's heart.

The best part? Watching lives change, like, actually change. Not just inside the church building but all over our community. People from every kind of background suddenly find out they're not alone. Turns out, we all want the same thing: connection, growth, and a reason to get up in the morning.

Community isn't just a buzzword. It's survival. It's family. And honestly? It's where we encounter Jesus daily.

Everything you've read up to this point has been intense. Some of it might have felt heavy or raw. But I need to make something clear: While God has allowed me to walk through painful and even sometimes devastating circumstances, He has also given me great teachers, grandparents full of wisdom, and mentors who held onto me tightly, many times when I was ready to let go.

Some of the guidance I've written in this book may sound bold or even presumptuous. After all, who am I to claim to know what the church should look like, what pastors and laity should be, or even what it means to follow a call? But I've lived this. I've been formed and re-formed by it. I've been broken by it and healed by it.

I've discovered that when I meet someone, whether they're a pastor, a lay leader, or someone far from God, I instinctively begin asking two questions: What is God's purpose for this person's life? And what is God's purpose for putting this person in my path? That's something I had not done often in my ministry. I was empathetic, I was there for people, and I prayed fervently for those under my care. But I had stopped walking slowly through the crowd.

The story from Matthew 9 took on new meaning for me. When the woman with the issue of blood desperately brushed the hem of Jesus' garment, He intentionally stopped to see her. Don't miss that. He wanted to SEE her. That is Jesus. I had convinced myself the model pastor wouldn't have time to see a person, just to keep my eye on the people. That was wrong. True community meant keeping the individual as primary. I had begun to focus on community as a crowd and almost forgot that community is made up of souls, individual souls who God desperately loves.

I don't always know the answer to the problems or questions that come at me as a pastor. Sometimes the revelation comes much later. But asking them keeps my eyes open. More importantly, it keeps my heart open. And that's how I've learned to lead: with open hands and an open heart. Not polished, but present.

It took a major shift for me. But it doesn't have to be that dramatic for you. For the first time in my adult life, there was no clear ministry assignment ahead. But the absence of clarity became an invitation to the stillness and out of the stillness came a new call.

I had long dreamed of planting a church. Over the years, I thought I had missed the window. "That's for younger pastors," I told myself. "That ship has sailed." But I came across a study that changed my mind: Studies into church planting have discovered that average church planter age has increased to a range of forties and fifties. This is because older church planters tend to be more prepared, come with deeper experience, have better support networks, and launch healthier churches that tend to be more successful over the long haul.[3] Maybe the dream wasn't dead, just delayed.

There's something uniquely humbling about starting over in your fifties. You have the benefit and the baggage of experience. You know what works, and you know the danger of trusting what works more than trusting God.

But I was ready to plant something different. Not just another church. A biblical community. A church that looks more like Acts 2 than a conference center. A church where pastors are shepherds, not CEOs. Where mission drives programs, not the other way around.

---

3. Aaron Earls, "Important Trends Among Church Plants and Multisite Campuses," *Lifeway Research*, September 30, 2022. Hansen, Collin. "Welcome Back, Church Planting." The Gospel Coalition. March 2026. https://www.thegospelcoalition.org/

When God called Joshua to lead the people into the Promised Land, He said, "Be strong and courageous." But He also said, "Meditate on [the Book of the Law] day and night… then you will be prosperous and successful" (Joshua 1:8). In other words, the success of the mission depended not on strategy but on surrender.

Our congregation chose our name because we believe grace doesn't just patch us up, it brings us back from the dead. This isn't a reboot. It's a rebirth.

And now, after decades of ministry, I'm finally beginning to understand what real pastoral leadership looks like. Again, not polished. Not perfect. But present. Let me say that one more time for good measure: not polished. Not perfect. But present.

So where do we go from here?

If you're a pastor or church leader, this is for you. But even if you're not, these are principles every follower of Christ can live by. This is not a model of success. This is the model of the Savior.

1. Let Vulnerability Become Your Strength

In a world of curated images and strategic branding, what people are dying for is someone real. Jesus did not hide His grief, His exhaustion, or His love. He wept. He got angry. He knelt. He washed feet. Vulnerability is not a liability. It's a pathway to trust.

When Joseph finally revealed his identity to his brothers in Genesis 45, he didn't lecture them. He wept so loudly that Pharaoh's house heard him. That's what redemption looks like. That's what real leadership looks like.

2. Preach With the People, Not at Them

Paul reminds the Corinthians that he came "not with wise and persuasive words, but with a demonstration of the Spirit's power" (1 Corinthians 2:4). Preaching is not performance. It's communion. Speak with your congregation. Share your life. Speak Scripture with tears in your eyes and conviction in your bones.

3. Stop Trying to Be Joshua. Let God Be Joshua

Pastors love Joshua. He's strong. He's victorious. He gets things done. But even Joshua bowed low. Even Joshua stopped listening. You are not the hero of the story; God is. And God's victories come on His timing, not yours.

4. Build Community, Not Just Crowds

Jesus had twelve. He could have had 1,200. But He chose to go deep. He taught in crowds, but He discipled in circles. Don't confuse attendance with transformation. Pastors, your greatest impact may come from the small table, not the large stage.

5. Chase Obedience, Not Optics

It's tempting to chase metrics. To look good on paper. But ask yourself: am I obedient? Am I doing what God asked me to do, even if no one sees it? Noah built a boat when no one had seen rain. Obedience matters more than optics.

REFLECTION FOR THE PASTOR'S HEART:

Where in your life are you chasing success instead of obedience?

Have you built spaces for vulnerability with your team and congregation?

Do you preach to impress or to impact?

Are you willing to walk away from platforms in order to follow Jesus more closely?

What would it look like to lead with open hands and an open heart?

You may not be a perfect pastor. But you can be a real one. And maybe that's the model the world needs most.

YOU ARE YOUR PASTOR'S KEEPER

The Christian army is the only army that shoots and buries its wounded.

–Dr. Freddie Gage

Dr. Gage's quote is hard to hear and even harder for me to write. In my years of ministry, I have found it to be painfully accurate. Pastors do unwise things and make mistakes. Most areas of vocation have processes in place to help in those situations. The church rarely does this well. Yet the church should be the model for the rest of the world. Christianity is the author of restoration, but 90 percent of the church is the worst at that very thing. Rather than reflecting Christ's model of redemptive restoration, some Christian communities have adopted responses to failure, exhaustion, and struggle that resemble expulsion more than healing.

It's a blessing and a burden to write this chapter, but it may be the most important chapter in the book. When Natalie and I decided to just sit with the Lord and wait for what was next for us, we came across two organizations that ministered deeply to our family. I was both saddened and elated that they even existed. One was Pastor's Hope out of Tyler, Texas, and the other was Care for Pastors in Leesburg, Florida. Both exist because when a pastor deals with a crisis in ministry or just moves on after being used up and worn out, the very people they have ministered to are usually nowhere to be found. Even worse, the pastor's family, who are innocents, lose their church and community overnight with nowhere to turn. In my opinion, we shouldn't need parachurch ministries to minister to pastors and their families in crisis. If we really believed and lived out the Christian faith, we would, despite the awkwardness and conflicting feelings those situations can bring, have a biblical plan to first, restore and second, walk with the clergy family in a way that honors God and the congregation.

I've seen the good, bad, and ugly sides of ministry. And the ugly is really ugly. I need to clearly say that when a pastor has committed a crime, separation of that pastor and the congregation is almost (almost) always imperative. But very few situations are that. A pastor's family's deep hurt most often is never healed because congregational leaders just won't or do not know how to follow, biblical principles in those times. Often, the ripple effect is devastating to many in ways we never know about. Many have lost their faith because of the poor handling of pastor/church conflicts. Again, this is not a defensive commentary against the local church but a clear picture of what is the reality and how Christian community can avoid these pitfalls and be excellent witnesses to unbelievers.

On any given week, Protestant pastors spend 15 hours in sermon prep, 7 hours meeting with congregants, 6.5 hours in email or correspondence, 4 hours meeting with staff, another 6.5 hours leading services and events, and about 5 hours in some sort of personal development.[1]

Pastors need more than just good intentions to do well in the ever-changing and often demanding life of church leadership. They need people around them who know how difficult it can be for them and are willing to help them stay strong, flexible, and complete. To support

---

1. Packiam, Glen, *The Resilient Pastor.* Baker Books, 2022, p. 49.

a pastor, you don't have to fix or manage them; you just have to walk with them with care, wisdom, and grace.

Life in the church these days is rarely predictable. Things that used to feel stable can change quickly, and pastors are often expected to stay calm and clear-headed in the middle of uncertainty. Patience with change is one of the best things a church can give.

Pastors can avoid the stress of having to keep things that don't help the mission by encouraging flexibility, giving people space to try new things, and supporting new ideas. Growth often means going into new places, and pastors need to know that they are not alone when they do.

Perspective also plays a role in good leadership. Pastors are better off when they are around people who value creativity, curiosity, and shared knowledge. When church members are open to new ideas, encourage people to work together, and give thoughtful feedback, they help make an environment where leaders can learn and grow instead of feeling alone.

No pastor can know everything. It helps both the leader and the church when they tell people to lean on others who have different strengths. It's important to have clear priorities. A lot of pastors take on too much, often because they care about their work and their people. Helping them focus on what really matters can change their lives. It's often better to do fewer things well than to do everything at once. Pastors should never be required to attend every church meeting or event on the calendar. As a matter of fact, that is ministerial malpractice. When church members step up, share responsibility, and support clear communication of vision, they help pastors lead with purpose instead of exhaustion.

Another thing to think about is passion. Ministry is very personal, and even the most dedicated leaders can lose their passion over time. Pastors can reconnect with what first called them to serve by people gently encouraging them to think, rest, and renew. Sometimes this means helping them realize when they are running out of energy and giving them permission to slow down, listen, and find joy again.

It's also important to recognize the special challenges that pastors face. They often put their own needs aside to help others through grief, conflict, and crisis. Empathy is very helpful. Just knowing how much emotional and spiritual weight they carry can change how support is given.

Every member of the church has a part to play, not as a critic but as an active partner in making sure their leader is healthy. Pastors may never say out loud how much they need consistent support, presence, and engagement. Community is where strong leaders shine. Ministry was never meant to be done alone. I want to reiterate here that almost every congregational crisis, moral failure, or broken policy is prefaced by lone ranger ministry.

When churches accept shared leadership and don't try to put everything on one person, pastors can lead in a way that lasts longer. To grow, you often have to move, and being afraid of change can be worse than taking careful steps forward. Like someone holding a ladder steady, the quiet, faithful support of church members lets pastors climb without worry.

Burnout is one area where help is very important. Pastors don't always see it in themselves, and even when they do, they might not want to talk about it. It's important to make a culture where people feel free to talk honestly. Simple check-ins, real concern, and a willingness to listen without judging can help people heal. Paying attention to changes in energy, mood, or interest lets you deal with problems before they get worse. Help that is useful is also important. Giving a pastor a break by volunteering time, sharing leadership, or doing things behind the scenes can really help. It's not a sign of weakness to suggest that people see a counselor, join a peer group, or use other helpful resources. It's a sign of wisdom.

Being recognized and thanked also feeds the soul. Taking the time to recognize milestones, celebrate faithfulness, and say thank you reminds pastors that their work is important and appreciated.

Another important part of a pastor's health is having healthy boundaries. Ministry can make it hard to tell the difference between work and personal life, especially when expectations aren't clear. Pastors can experience longer, healthier tenures when churches openly support the importance of rest, family time, and personal space. Respecting office hours, limiting contact after hours or on days off, and encouraging time away show that you care and trust the other person. When pastors are helped to set limits, they can be their best selves when they are there. It's not a luxury to take breaks and have time for yourself. They are important. Without them, you get tired, lose your creativity, and have trouble making decisions. Taking time off lets pastors rest, think, and reconnect with God, their families, and themselves. These breaks often help people see things in a new way and understand their pastors better. They also make relationships stronger, both inside the home and outside of the church. When pastors show how to have healthy cycles of rest and renewal, they give others the freedom to do the same. This helps create a church culture that values being whole over being busy all the time. Service, silence, prayer, and personal renewal all help spiritual growth. Taking time for these things makes faith stronger and leadership better. Taking good care of pastors is an act of faithfulness for the whole church in the end. Everyone benefits when leaders are supported, respected, and encouraged to have a balanced life. When people choose to work together, healthy churches are built. Healthy pastors can lead with clarity, compassion, and joy.

No pastor can or should try to shoulder a church alone. Healthy ministries are made one day at a time by folks like you: everyday people who choose to love well. Your pastor may be your senior leader on staff. But again, you are the one holding the ladder that allows them to reach higher and farther. When church members know how to rally behind their leadership and refuse to let them go it alone, everyone benefits. Pastors can stay full. The church can continue to grow. Ministry becomes life giving instead of exhausting. In this chapter, I want to address the single most important person in the ministry of your local church…YOU! If you've read this far and you're not a vocational pastor, congratulations! You're exactly who God is developing right now to walk alongside your pastor. To hold up their arms when they're tired. To be the voice of reason that they so very often don't have. Listen up. When you finish reading these paragraphs, you'll understand why.

What I have to say next is straight from my heart and I think the heart of a holy God. You can no longer hide behind ignorance. Your pastor needs your bravery, your patience, and your giftings. They may also need you to firmly, lovingly speak the truth to them in love. God works through church leaders to give the pastor permission and support to practice the gifts God has given them and to "equip the saints for the work of ministry" (Ephesians 4:12 ESV). Let's walk through how you, layperson or church leader, play such an important role in keeping pastors healthy and strong. It won't happen because they feel guilty. Or because you pressure them. But it can happen because of grace, love, and mercy. Afterall, that's exactly what Jesus has given you and what most pastors give out to their congregations daily.

This is NOT just a nuts-and-bolts way to support you pastors. This is a calling. When Moses got tired in battle, Aaron and Hur held up his arms so that the people would win (Exodus 17:12). That is the visual I want you to imagine. You are holding the ladder or holding up the arms, and not only are you holding them, but you're also strengthening them. Let's get practical. Pray for your pastor by name. Stop gossiping about your pastor. Serve without being asked. YOU are not on the sidelines of ministry watching it happen. YOU are part of the supernatural equation of the church.

People change. Seasons of life change. The church has constantly evolving needs. For the lead pastor or senior pastor, the environment of their ministry will never look the same two days in a row, and your leadership team should remain fluid as well. As Christians, we are called to love God by loving those around us where they are. That means pastors shouldn't cling to old ways if the current situation calls for a new approach. They need the freedom to adapt, to shift, and to grow. YOU can help or hinder that process. Stop expecting your pastor to stand still when everyone around them is evolving.

Change is scary. But leaning into the unknown with your pastor will empower them to lead your church into the future.

SUPPORTING HEALTHY PASTORS: KEY INSIGHTS FOR CHURCH MEMBERS

In the dynamic and challenging world of church leadership, it's essential to empower pastors to be resilient, adaptive, and thriving leaders. Here's how you can support their journey:

Lean Into the Unknown

Leadership is a risk. There is no scenario where your senior pastor will ever know all the variables and make a decision with 100 percent certainty. You can empower them and choose to trust. When circumstances change or your leader has to make a hard decision with limited information, offer grace. Assume positive intent. Choose to believe he or she is asking for wisdom, even if you don't have all the details figured out. Yes, it may seem high risk, but pastors should be constantly pushing the envelope and growing in new areas to reach more people with the love of Jesus. Often, parishioners who have control issues or certain preferences actually keep a pastor *from* fulfilling the Great Commission.

But what about when your pastor needs to do something new to reach you? Support them. Allow them to miscalculate or fail. Failing forward is the norm for clergy leaders. Ministry is often trial and error. As long as everyone assumes the goal is to grow current Christ-followers and gain new ones, anything is fixable and redeemable. When your leader steps out of their comfort zone to learn, grow, and develop in areas that will benefit the church as a whole, you have two options. You can belittle or shame them for not knowing how to do it all. Or you can celebrate that they are stepping out of a comfort zone for the greater good of those they serve. Please, please choose the latter. Never allow a pastor to cater to the needs of an individual or a few. In ministry, what's best for the whole is always a truly called pastor's goal.

Trusting your leader is putting your faith into action. Proverbs 3:5 tells us to trust in the Lord with all our heart. Part of trusting God with all your heart is trusting the leaders that He has placed in your life. Here are some practical ways to demonstrate trust:

- Resist the urge to complain when something shocks you.

- Volunteer for the new initiative instead of waiting for proof of success.

- Send them a message that says, 'I don't have all the answers either, but I am praying for wisdom and courage for you.'

- Let your pastor know you are only there to help and encourage. Never support your pastor while in their presence while showing that you are not supportive when they are not in the room.

Allow Others to Speak

Your pastor should not have to hear every single person's opinion or idea. Nor should they try to. Part of being a wise leader is stepping back and allowing others to lead when they have special knowledge or expertise. We see an example of this in Moses. Moses was taught by God and his father-in-law, Jethro, that he needed to allow others to lead.

> *What you are doing is not good. You and these people who come to you will only wear yourselves out. The work is too heavy for you; you cannot handle it alone. Listen now to me and I will give you some advice, and may God be with you.... Teach them his decrees and instructions, and show them the way they are to live and how they are to behave. But select capable men from all the people—men who fear God, trustworthy men who hate dishonest gain... That will make your load lighter, because they will share it with you. If you do this and God so commands, you will be able to stand the strain, and all these people will go home satisfied.*
>
> *–Exodus 18:17–23*

You can apply this to your church by praising your pastor when they allow others to lead. Speak life over your staff and ministry leaders. If you have insight to offer, do so graciously and in the right time and setting. Encourage your pastor to allow others to lead when necessary.

Ask Questions

Pastors thrive on conversation. When two or more are gathered, they hear different perspectives and consider opinions they may never have thought of on their own. Pastors like hearing your thoughts, ideas, and concerns (as long as they are presented in a respectful way). Allowing your pastor to hear from the people in your church helps them make wiser decisions. So, encourage them to ask questions.

James 1:19 commands us to be quick to listen and slow to speak. When you ask questions, make sure you're asking them in order to understand. Don't go into a conversation with assumptions. If you are unclear about something or a decision, say, "Help me understand why you think this is a good idea. Here is my idea." But only if you're willing to do it. Let your pastor know that you care about what they think. Asking questions orients the conversation back to your pastor and can strengthen your relationship and give them the confidence they need to follow God's leading and not that of a strong personality.

Listen to Experts

While your pastor is an expert in theology and shepherding your church, there are other areas of your church that your pastor does not know everything about. Your pastor may not know the ins-and-outs of technology, small group structure, or how to best utilize communication platforms. If your pastor asks questions or brings in someone with special knowledge to help your church, that is a wonderful thing. Celebrate when your leader surrounds himself with smart people. Your pastor knows they don't know it all. Encourage them to lean on experts, then allow them to lead when it comes to those subjects.

Proverbs 11:14 tells us that there is victory in many advisers. If you're an expert at something, offer your help. If someone else is brought in to help your church, welcome them with open arms. Don't be threatened by others' expertise. A healthy church celebrates wisdom wherever it comes from.

Welcome Input from Volunteers and Staff

Your pastor should not only welcome input from other staff members but also from key volunteers and leaders in your church. A church will never be healthy if they think they are the only one whose opinion matters. Make sure your pastor knows it's okay to take criticism from the church family. When they feel comfortable delegating and allowing others to lead portions of the church, they will never feel burnt out from trying to do it all.

There are many different gifts in Romans 12, and they all work together. You can apply this to your church by being reliable. If you commit to doing something on staff or as a volunteer, do it. If you have something to say about an idea your pastor has, say it in love and perhaps offline. When others see you as reliable, they will offer the same courtesy to your pastor.

Remember Your Why

Churches will grow weary if they try to do it all. At some point, your pastor will have to say no to continue to support the health of your church. Challenge your pastor to regularly evaluate weekly activities, events, and programs with your church vision and mission in mind. When something no longer aligns with the direction you're trying to head, it can easily be let go of with no regret.

Hebrews 12:1 tells us to throw off what slows us down. Help your pastor let go of attachments to events and programs that are no longer benefiting the church. When something comes to an end, thank God for the season it served, but don't look back. Each time you allow something to go, you are making room for new fruit to grow.

Keep the Main Thing the Main Thing

One of the best ways you can keep your pastor focused on why your church does what they do is to HAVE A CLEAR VISION. When the 'why' of your church is simple and straight to the point, there is no room for unnecessary, distracting activities. This also allows pastors to spend less time explaining their decisions because you will be united on the 'why' behind them. You can protect your leader from busy work by reminding them (and yourself!) of the church's 'why.'

Jesus had a focus on why He did what He did: "For the Son of Man has come to seek and to save that which was lost" (Luke 19:10 NASB). You can remind your pastor of your vision by frequently talking about it. When conflicts arise, refer to your shared vision. When the 'why' is clear, your pastor will experience less friction.

Guard Your Pastor's Passion

Pastors slowly lose their passion. They wake up one day and realize they forgot to enjoy what they love to do. They can't quite identify the point it all went south, but they know it happened. One of the best ways you can support your pastor is by guarding their fuel.

Encouragement fuels passion. Galatians 6:9 says don't grow weary while doing good. Tell your pastor how their leadership has impacted you. Tell them stories. Pray with them that God would renew their joy. Before you know it, passion will return when you fill their tank with gratitude.

Celebrate Your Pastor's Wins Publicly

Sit down with your pastor every once in a while and really listen to what they have to say. Ask what they enjoy about ministry. What brings them passion? When their eyes light up while talking about something unusual God is doing in your church, celebrate with them. It might take some time for your pastor to rediscover what they love about being a pastor, but praising God with your pastor for the good things that happen will allow you both to recognize it when the inevitable struggles come along.

Philippians 4:8 says to let our thoughts dwell on what is praiseworthy. Make celebrating God-moments a regular thing in your life. Leave your pastor notes. Thank the pastors at your church. When you make gratitude a habit, your pastor will notice and thrive.

Know When to Speak Up

Pastors are more positive and energetic when they get to serve the church around their primary gifts. However, if your pastor has gone from normally loving and joyful to short-tempered, withdrawn, or chronically exhausted, something is wrong, either stress, unresolved conflict, or maybe something deeper. Don't wait for your pastor to ask for help. Ask them if they're okay. Many pastors won't voice concerns until they feel depleted. Give them the opportunity to open up before it becomes damaging.

Galatians 6:2 reminds us to bear one another's burdens. Ask your pastor how you can help. Pray with them. Encourage them to take a break or seek counseling if they need it. Often pastors feel there is a stigma if they seek out therapy or counseling. Assure them it's healthy and honoring to God. Even better, establish a fund for staff to use to pay for attending to their mental health. Speaking into your pastor's life doesn't always have to be positive. When we love our pastors well, we may offer gentle confrontation.

Schedule Quiet Time

Many pastors have their best thoughts and teaching come to them when they take time away from the chaos. Creativity often does not come at their desk in their office. If your lead pastor needs to be reminded to schedule rest into their life, encourage them to step away, slow down, and just be with God.

Psalm 46:10 commands us to be still and know that He is God. Offer to watch their kids for a date night. Gift them with a retreat day. Encourage them to be like Christ and get away consistently to "lonely places" (Luke 5:16).

Rest is Worship

In today's world, taking a break seems selfish. In my early years of ministry, I felt guilty for taking vacations or breaks. Unfortunately, there were church leaders who frowned upon consistent time off. This is unchristian and dangerous. Keeping the Sabbath is fulfilling the fourth commandment. Pastors need to be told, given permission, and held accountable to schedule quiet months or vacations. Pastors need rest. The church needs rest. If we lead teams that take regular time away from church, we will all be better and stronger for it. Encourage silent retreats and continuing education, and budget expenses for both the pastor and their spouse to travel together during these times. A pastor's spouse is often under the same and sometimes more pressure as a public figure in the church.

Jesus took breaks to pray (Luke 5:16). Give your pastor permission to rest by protecting their day off. Speak positively about them taking a sabbatical. Remember that God can and will continue to take care of the church when they are resting.

Take Vacation

Pastors should not feel guilty when they take vacations to restore their souls and spend time with their family. If you know your leader is going to be unplugging from the world for a bit, encourage them to do it. They need time away to gain perspective.

When your pastor takes vacation, allow them to truly unplug by serving in their absence. Welcome them back from vacation. Don't slander them when they take needed time away. You'll be surprised how well your pastor leads when they regularly REST.

Put Family First

Pastors sometimes also feel guilty when they spend concentrated time with their family. Whether that is taking their kid to soccer practice or taking a day to celebrate their anniversary, pastors need to make family a priority. If they don't spend quality time with their family, they will have nothing left to give their church. Some of the most committed atheists are pastors' kids who grew up in churches where the pastor's family was rarely even considered an afterthought. Remind them that family comes first.

1 Timothy 3 tells us that a leader must take care of their home and family. Encourage your pastor to make family time a priority.

Speak life over their spouse. When your pastor's home life is in order, you'll watch their ministry exponentially grow, and you provide care for their family as well.

Pay Your Pastor a Fair Salary

Pastors often live below or just a bit above the poverty level. They often have student loan debts related to their call to and equipping for ministry. Financial struggles combining with the normal stresses of ministry can be a dangerous formula. Don't live by the old way of "keeping the pastor humble." That is against everything God meant for his servants. A fair wage communicates trust and respect. It's an investment for the future of your congregation and fulfills Paul's words in 1 Timothy 5:19.

EPILOGUE

The present pastor, I've learned, is the pastor who is fully engaged in the lives of his or her parishioners. Because there are appropriate boundaries and care for people in various stages of mental health, it is difficult to know how to be present and how much to be present. But I believe Jesus is our best example. Jesus was always in the moment; He fully and unconditionally loved even the worst sinners and listened to them intently before advising them.

The polished pastor is a loaded term I know. What's a "good" trait to one person can absolutely be "bad" to another. It can be confusing because the American version of pastoring has gone through many evolutionary changes. In the early centuries of America, a pastor was usually known as a humble, often poor and in general, not well-educated, kind, and prayerful soul. In the early 1900s, transportation became easier and revivalists or tent preachers could take their church on the road, so to speak. Immigrants came from all over the world and brought their practices of Christianity, and as the world of the church grew, so did the pressure to compete and function as the president or CEO of a congregation, especially those which included more prominent members of the community. There was a rise in preachers being affected by more respect, celebrity, and higher salaries. Pastors who were playing a role more than fulfilling a call began to enter pulpits as religion became a deeper part of the fabric of society.

I've always been fascinated by the book *Elmer Gantry* by Sinclair Lewis. Most pastors would never admit it, but I've always found the fictitious story bore enough truth that it helped to keep me on track and check my own temptations. It's an insightful commentary on the human ego. Released in 1927, it highlights the antics of a pastor who was well aware of his congregation's expectations that he fit the role of a respected community leader. He learns quickly that the expectations far surpass basic pastoral care and a good sermon once a week.

I remember as a young pastor reading this book in seminary, and I've never forgotten a quote that sums it up and carries over well into the twenty-first century. In describing the pastor's discoveries about leading a church, Lewis says, "He had learned how to assemble Jewish texts, Greek philosophy, and Middle-Western evangelistic anecdotes into a sermon. And he had learned that poverty was blessed, but that bankers make the best deacons."[1]

The professional pastor has been molded and formed more by cultural standards than biblical call. They pastor out of the mindset of how things should be, what they should sound like, and how the church should perform. Ministry eventually becomes more of a position to manage than people to care for. As leadership shifts into CEO or manager mode, presence is typically the first thing to go. Hours are spent preaching, planning, and programming *in front of* people rather than *with* them. Prayer becomes more about asking people to fill seats rather than providing covers for those in need. The call to lay down our lives in humble service is exchanged for a list of metrics, optics, and control. What was designed by God to be poured out on others is defended as a position to protect.

Present pastors lead radically differently. They lead by being physically, visibly, and verbally present with the people they've been called to serve. A present pastor spends less time trying to appear effective and more time actually being effective by showing up. They

---

1. Lewis, Sinclair. *Elmer Gantry* (Harcourt, Brace and Company), 1927, *pg. 221.*

understand that presence is better than polish. They know people need to hear your voice as well as your sermon. Death, life, and divorce are not delegated or avoided; you walk with your people through it. The present pastor recognizes the apostle Paul's words to the church in Philippi and understands they are called to be a shepherd, not a manager. They smell like their sheep because they are present with their sheep.

Another major difference is how a pastor leads. Pastors who are present lead with truth and honesty, but that truth is molded by love not judgment. These pastors view people as children of God first, rather than seeing donors, volunteers, or church supporters. They give advice without condemnation and hold people accountable without shame. They refuse to entertain an Americanized Christianity where parishioner relationships are determined by their bank account, family ties, or social media following. They lead like Jesus by modeling what it looks like to have a servant's heart through sacrifice, humility, and most importantly, faithfulness.

The professional pastor has learned to focus on being defined by pews, programs, and potlucks, and culture has helped us to be more faithful to our Sunday schedule than we are to Christ. The CEO teaches that church attendance equals obedience. For many years in ministry, I'm embarrassed to say, I equated being a "good pastor" with God being impressed that I put on a suit, walked into a building, and led my congregations to sing three songs before the sermon. Let me tell you something that will shatter every shallow assumption you've been clinging to: God is not fooled by our routine. God is not impressed by our ritual, and God is not glorified by our financial statistics. He demands your obedience to the call we've answered to preach the Gospel to all, baptizing them in the name of the Father, the Son, and the Holy Spirit.

We are living in an age of religious deception where millions have been inoculated against the true Gospel by watered-down sermons, emotional music, and the lie that just going to church means knowing the true Christ. In my professional mode, I nurtured that. You sit in a pew. You nod at the sermon. I went home content on Sunday afternoons because my sanctuary was full. I became uninterested that people remained unchanged. Why? I allowed my spirit to be assaulted by the pursuit of creating fans of religious culture. The Pharisees went to the synagogue. They tithed. They fasted. They knew the scriptures better than most pastors today, and yet Jesus said to them, "You belong to your father, the devil." (John 8:44) Why? Because their hearts were unrepentant. They loved the appearance of holiness, not the reality of it. They clung to the structure but rejected the Spirit.

I finally began to look at myself in the mirror and came to terms with the fact that I wasn't worried about being less present because my numbers were gaining me accolades with my congregation and Bishop. They were not the problem; I was. I had traded presence and servanthood for professionalism and performance. Everything about how I do ministry changed when I made the decision to be present, slowed down, and began asking the two questions: What is God's purpose for this person's life? And what is God's purpose for putting this person in my path?

It is my prayer that you will choose presence over polish. The Kingdom depends on it.

SCAN HERE to learn more about
Invite Ministries—created to invite people to a deeper
faith and living relationship with Jesus Christ